Self-Love for Teen Girls

An Empowering Guide to Build a Positive Self-image, Unlock Your Inner Power, Improve Social Skills, Fight Peer Pressure, Overcome Stress & Anxiety, and Set Firm Boundaries.

Jacqueline D. Austin

Manufactured in: USA

Cover Art: DANIELLE REES

Interior Design: DANIELLE REES

Art Producer: BROOKE WHITE

Production Editor: SIENNA ADAMS

Production Manager: SARAH JOHNSON

Editor: AALIYAH LYONS

Photography: MICHAEL SMITH

Table Of Contents

Introduction

Welcome to a journey like no other — a journey that is completely about you. It's a journey of self-discovery, empowerment, and in particular, self-love. As you grasp this book, know that it's something other than words on a page. It's a partner in disguise, an aide, and a companion who will stroll with you as you explore the often complex and confusing world of being a teen girl. You are remaining at an extraordinary point in your life. Immaturity is a period of unbelievable change, development, and self-investigation. It's the point at which you're beginning to sort out what your identity is and who you need to turn into. But on the other hand, this period can feel overpowering, loaded up with pressures from school, companions, family, and society. There's so much going on, and in some cases, neglecting to focus on yourself amidst everything can be a common thing, that is where this book comes in.

This isn't simply a book about self-love — it's a book about revolution. A revolution that begins with you, a revolution that challenges the negative messages you could have caught wind of yourself, that stands up against the tensions to adjust, and that engages you to embrace who you genuinely and truly are.

But what does it mean to love yourself? and why is it so important? These are the questions we'll explore together. We'll talk about what self-love really means—beyond the hashtags, beyond the Instagram posts, and beyond the surface-level advice that's often thrown your way. We'll delve deeper, on more meaningful aspects of self-love, the kind that has the power to transform your life from the inside out. As you set out on this journey. I believe that you should recall a certain something: You are sufficient. Similarly, as you are on the spot. You don't have to change who you are to deserve love, regard, and bliss. You as of now have all that you want inside you. This book is here to assist you with finding that, to assist you with discovering the magnificence, strength, beauty and possibility that exists within.

Let's face it: being a teenager can be tough. There are moments of pure joy and freedom, like when you're hanging out with friends, exploring new hobbies, or just being your fabulous self.

But there are also times when you might feel overwhelmed, unsure, or even a little lost. Maybe you're struggling with self-doubt, facing peer pressure, or trying to balance the expectations of school, family, and your social life or maybe you're simply trying to figure out where you fit in this big wide world. Whatever challenges you're facing know that you're not alone. This book is here to remind you that you have the power to navigate through these challenges and come out stronger, wiser, and more in tune with who you are. You are capable of incredible things and this journey is all about unlocking that potential. As you read through these pages, you'll find practical advice, empowering exercises, and inspiring stories designed to help you build self-love, develop a positive self-image, and live your life with confidence and purpose. But more than that you'll find a space where you can be yourself—where you can explore your thoughts, feelings, and dreams without judgment. This is your journey and it's one worth embracing with open arms.

So, take a deep breath, grab a cozy spot and let's dive in. Remember, this isn't just a book—it's a conversation. I'm here with you. cheering you on every step of the way. Together, we're going to explore what it means to truly love yourself, to overcome the obstacles in your path, and to live a life that's authentically and beautifully yours.

Presently, we should discuss what this book is and how this will help you on your journey of "Self-Love For Teen Girls-An Empowering Guide to Build a Positive Self-Image, Unlock Your Inner Power, Improve Social Skills, Fight Peer Pressure, Overcome Stress & Anxiety, and Set Firm Boundaries" is something beyond an assortment of guidance — it's a plan for building a day-to-day existence that you love, from the back to front. The thought for this book was conceived out of a simple yet powerful realization: that the journey to self-love and empowerment is one of the main journey's you'll at any point take.This journey will shape what your identity is, the manner in which you see the world, and how you carry on with your life. What's more, it's a journey where each girl has the right to live with certainty, support, and a feeling of direction. This book is separated into seven sections, each zeroing in on an alternate part of self-love and self-improvement. We'll begin by investigating the idea of self-love — What is it? Why is it important? and the way that it can change your life. From that point, we'll plunge into subjects like fostering a positive self-picture, opening your inward power, serious areas of strength for building abilities, and exploring the tensions and difficulties of being a teen.

Be that as it may. This book isn't just about hypothesis — it's about activity. All through every section, you'll track down practical tips, exercises, and journaling prompts intended to assist you with incorporating what you've realized. These tools are here to help you dig deep, reflect on your experiences, and make real, lasting changes in your life. You'll likewise find stories and models from different girls who have strolled this way before you. Their encounters will show you that you're in good company, that the difficulties you face are shared by quite a few people, and that there is dependably a way forward. These accounts are here to rouse you, to tell you that your part of a larger community of girls and women who are on their own journey of self-discovery and empowerment. Also, Here's the most outstanding aspect: this journey doesn't have an endpoint. It's a long-lasting course of learning, growing, and evolving.

As you go through this book, you'll gain tools and insights that will serve you not just now, but for years to come. You'll figure out how to embrace your uniqueness, how to support yourself, and how to carry on with a life that is consistent with what your identity is. This book is a challenge to step into your power, to perceive your value, and to carry on with your existence with certainty and happiness. It's a reminder that you are sufficient, similarly as you are, and that you have all that you want inside you to make a daily existence that you love. Anyway, what do you say? Could it be said that you are prepared to set out on this journey of self-love and empowerment? Is it true that you are prepared to find it? Survive and embrace the astounding individual you are? How about we get everything rolling!

This book is more than just something to read—it's a tool for transformation. To get the most out of it. I encourage you to approach it with an open heart and mind. Here are a few tips on how to use this book effectively:

- There's no rush to get through this book. Take your time with each chapter, allowing yourself to fully absorb the information and reflect on how it applies to your life.
- As you read, keep a journal where you can write down your thoughts, feelings, and insights. This will help you process what you're learning and track your growth over time.
- Throughout the book, you'll find exercises and prompts designed to help you apply what you're learning. Don't skip these! They are an essential part of the process and will help you integrate the lessons into your life.
- As you work through the book, take time to reflect on your progress. Revisit chapters or exercises that resonate with you and don't be afraid to spend extra time on areas where you feel you need more growth.
- Consider sharing what you're learning with a trusted friend, family member, or mentor. Talking about your experiences can provide additional support and insight and it can also help you stay accountable to your goals.

Importance Of Empowerment and Self-Love

Let us firstly understand the concept of empowerment. Empowerment is a term that is frequently utilized, yet what does it truly mean? At its core, empowerment is tied in with acquiring certainty, information, and solidarity to assume command over your life. It's tied in with understanding that you have the ability to settle on your own decisions, to defend yourself, and to make the existence you need. For the majority of teen girls, empowerment starts with understanding and embracing your own value.

At the point when you perceive that you are important. Competent, and deserving of happiness, you begin to distinctively see the world. You begin to settle on decisions that line up with your qualities and your objectives, as opposed to simply attempting to fit in or satisfy others. Empowerment isn't something that works out more or less by accident — it's a cycle. It requires self-mindfulness, fortitude, and a promise to self-improvement. It's tied in with perceiving that you have the ability to mold your life, and that you don't need to hang tight for another person to allow you to act naturally. Self-love is the foundation of empowerment. Without self-love, becoming influenced with the assessments and assumptions of others is easy. You could end up constantly looking for approval from outer sources — whether it's from companions. Family, or social media. However, when you love yourself, you begin to track down that validation from your inner soul. You start to consider yourself to be commendable and deserving of love, regard, and achievement. Self-love isn't tied in with being selfish or haughty. It's tied in with recognizing your assets, tolerating your defects, and treating yourself with the very empathy and care that you would propose to a companion. It's tied in with understanding that you should be blissful, and that you should have the ability to make a daily life that gives you pleasure and satisfaction.

"Empowerment Through Self-Love" - Empowerment and self-love are profoundly interconnected. At the point when you love yourself, you begin to feel more enabled to assume command over your life. You become more positive about simply deciding, defining limits, and chasing after your fantasies.

You begin to consider difficulties to be open doors for development, as opposed to snags that keep you down. This book is intended to assist you with both developing self-love and empowerment. As you work through the chapters, you'll gain the tools and insights you need to build a strong foundation of self-love, and you'll learn how to use that foundation to create a life that reflects your true self.

At the point when you practice self-love, it doesn't simply help you — it benefits everybody around you. At the point when you feel sure and secure in yourself, you're bound to treat others with benevolence and regard. You're stronger notwithstanding difficulties, and you're better prepared to help and elevate people around you. Along these lines, self-love makes an expanding influence, spreading inspiration and empowerment to everybody you connect with. As you develop self-love, you'll see changes in the manner in which you see yourself and the world. You'll begin to draw in good encounters and connections, and you'll feel more certain about chasing after your objectives. So, as you move forward. Remember this: You are powerful, You are worthy, and You have everything you need within you to create life that you love. Let this be your mantra, your guiding star and the foundation upon which you build your journey of self-discovery and personal growth.

How to Apply What You Learn From This Book

"Take Action" - As you read each chapter, think about how you can apply the lessons to your daily life. For example, if you're learning about self-awareness, take some time each day to reflect on your thoughts and feelings. If you're working on building self-compassion, practice being kind to yourself, especially when you make mistakes.
"Make an Everyday Practice" - Consistency is key with regards to self-awareness. Attempt to make a day to day or week after week schedule where you integrate the practices and activities from this book. Whether it's carving out opportunities for journaling, rehearsing care, or defining objectives. Having a routine will help you stay on track.
"Self-improvement is a lifelong journey" - It's vital to remain focused on the interaction in any event, while it's challenging. Recollect that it's alright to make little strides and that each forward-moving step is progress. Intermittently, find an opportunity to consider your advancement. Glance back at where you began and perceive how far you've come. This reflection will assist you with remaining motivated and focused on your objectives. While this book offers guidance and advice. It's important to remember that your journey is unique to you. Take what resonates with you, and feel free to adapt the lessons to fit your own needs and circumstances. For example, if a certain exercise doesn't feel right for you, try modifying it to better suit your style. If a particular concept resonates with you, spend more time exploring it and incorporating it into your life. The goal is to create a personalized approach to self-love and empowerment that works for you.

Chapter 1

Discovering The Mystique Of Your Inner Beauty

Self-love is one of the most significant, yet frequently misjudged, ideas in our lives. It's not just about pampering yourself with spa days, indulging yourself with something uniquely great, or carving out opportunities to unwind — however those things can be a piece of it. Self-love is a lot deeper. It's about how you see yourself, how you treat yourself, and the relationship you have with who you are at your core. At its pith, self-love is the acknowledgment that you are intrinsically important and deserving of love and respect, essentially in light of the fact that you simply exist. It's the comprehension that your value isn't dependent upon your accomplishments, your appearance, or the assessments of others. It's tied in with embracing what your identity is — defects and all — and treating yourself with a similar graciousness, sympathy, and understanding that you would propose to a dear companion.

SELF-LOVE IS A RELATIONSHIP WITH YOURSELF

Consider self-love the groundwork of your relationship with yourself. Very much like some other relationship. It requires consideration, care, and nurturing. At the point when you love somebody, you need what's best for them, you pardon their missteps, and you support their development and satisfaction. The equivalent goes for self-love. It's tied in with being your own greatest ally, your own wellspring of consolation, and your own place of refuge. This relationship with yourself is the main one you will at any point have in light of the fact that it impacts each and every relationship in your life. At the point when you have serious areas of strength for self-love, you set the norm for how others treat you. You're less inclined to endure undesirable connections or ways of behaving in light of the fact that you know your value. You likewise become more caring and understanding toward others since you're not working from a position of instability or need.

DEBUNKING MYTHS ABOUT SELF-LOVE

"Self-love is selfish"- One of the most common misconceptions is that self-love is selfish or self-focused. This couldn't possibly be more off-base. Self-love isn't tied in with placing yourself above others or dismissing their requirements, it's tied in with ensuring you're dealing with yourself so you can appear as the best version of yourself for other people. At the point when your cup is full, you have greater toity to give.

"Self-love means you never struggle with self-doubt"- Self-love doesn't imply that you're dependably sure or that you never experience self-question. It's not unexpected to have minutes where you feel unreliable or second guess yourself. Self-love is about how you answer those minutes. Rather than spiraling into pessimistic self-talk or self-analysis, you recognize your sentiments, show yourself empathy, and help yourself to remember your inborn worth.

"Self-love is about perfection"- Self-love isn't tied in with taking a stab at flawlessness or cherishing yourself just when you fulfill specific guidelines. It's tied in with embracing your blemishes and understanding that they are a piece of what makes you one of a kind and human. It's tied in with giving yourself effortlessness and realizing that you genuinely deserve love and respect, even when you commit errors or miss the mark concerning your own assumptions.

"Why Does Self-Love Matters"- At the point when you love yourself, you're better prepared to deal with life's difficulties with versatility and beauty. You're bound to focus on your psychological and emotional health, set healthy boundaries, and look for help when you want it. Self-love goes about as a cradle against the adverse consequences of stress, uneasiness, and wretchedness, permitting you to explore life with a more prominent feeling of harmony and equilibrium. As referenced before, your relationship with yourself establishes the vibe for your associations with others. When you have a strong foundation of self-love, you're less likely to tolerate unhealthy or toxic relationships. You draw in and develop connections that depend on shared respect, love, and understanding. You're additionally ready to give and get love all the more uninhibitedly on the grounds that you're not continually looking for approval from others. At the point when you love yourself, you're bound to put resources into your self-awareness and advancement. You're available to learn new things, facing challenges, and getting out of your usual range of familiarity since you have faith in your capacity to develop and advance. Self-love gives you the certainty to seek after your interests, put forth aggressive objectives, and make a life that lines up with your qualities and wants. Self-love also has a positive impact on your physical health. When you love yourself, you're more likely to take care of your body, nourish it with healthy foods, and engage in regular physical activity. You're also more likely to prioritize rest and relaxation, understanding that your body needs time to recharge and rejuvenate.

A Journey To Self-Love

Developing self-love is a journey, not an objective. It's a long-lasting course of learning, growing, and evolving. There will be times when you feel completely in line with yourself and other times when you battle to rehearse self-love. That is completely fine. What makes a difference is that you stay focused on the journey and keep on appearing for yourself, in any event, when it's difficult.

PRACTICE SELF-COMPASSION

Self-compassion is the foundation of self-love. It's tied in with treating yourself with a similar generosity, understanding. and care that you would propose to a companion. At the point when you commit an error or face a tough spot. practice self-compassion by recognizing your sentiments, advising yourself that it's OK to be flawed, and offering yourself uplifting statements and support.

CHALLENGE NEGATIVE SELF-TALK

We as a whole have an inner critic that can in some cases be brutal and critical. One of the main parts of self-love is figuring out how to challenge and reevaluate negative self-talk. At the point when you discover yourself thinking negative contemplations about yourself, stop and inquire as to whether those considerations are valid or supportive. Supplant them with positive confirmations or tokens of your assets and achievements.

SET HEALTHY BOUNDARIES

Setting sound limits is a fundamental piece of self-love. It's tied in with perceiving your requirements and cutoff points and imparting them to other people. Boundaries safeguard your time, energy, and prosperity, permitting you to focus on what means quite a bit to you. Defining limits can be challenging, if you're used to putting others' needs before your own, yet it's a significant stage in developing self-love.

NURTURE YOUR BODY

Your body is a sanctuary, and dealing with it is a strong demonstration of self-love. Set aside a few minutes for customary active work, eat supporting food varieties, and get sufficient rest. Stand by listening to your body and give it what it needs to flourish. Recollect that self-love isn't tied in with rebuffing your body or driving it to fit a specific form — it's about honoring and respecting it as it is.

PRIORITIZE YOUR WELL-BEING AND SUR-ROUND YOURSELF WITH POSITIVE INFLUENCE

Self-love implies focusing on your prosperity. This incorporates dealing with your psychology, profound, and actual wellbeing, as well as setting aside a few minutes for exercises that give you pleasure and satisfaction. It's tied in with tracking down a harmony between work, rest, and play, and ensuring that you're not continually forfeiting your requirements for other people. Individuals you encircle yourself with altogether affect your self-love journey. Encircle yourself with individuals who elevate, support, and empower you. Distance yourself from those who drain your energy or make you feel less than. Search out connections that depend on common regard. love, and understanding. Take time to celebrate your accomplishments, both big and small. Perceive your advancement and give yourself credit for the difficult work you've placed in. Commending your achievements supports your healthy identity worth and persuades you to keep developing and advancing.

A JOURNEY OF SELF-DISCOVERY

Self-discovery is a basic piece of understanding and cherishing yourself. It's the method involved with uncovering who you really are past the names and assumptions put on you by others. This journey isn't generally direct, it very well may be loaded up with exciting bends in the road as you investigate various parts of your personality and values. During puberty, you're in a period of quick change. Your inclinations, convictions, and objectives could move often as you gain new encounters and bits of knowledge. Embracing this journey implies being available to change and development, and understanding that it's alright to advance as you dive more deeply into yourself. Self-discovery includes posing yourself with significant inquiries and thinking about your responses. It implies investigating what fulfills you, what you're enthusiastic about, and what you esteem most throughout everyday life. This investigation can be both invigorating and overwhelming. However, it's fundamental for building a strong foundation of self-love.

- Writing about your thoughts, feelings, and experiences can provide valuable insights into who you are. Regular journaling helps you track your growth and understand your reactions to various situations.
- Take time to reflect on your experiences and how they have shaped you. Ask yourself questions like, "What have I learned from this experience?" or "How did I feel about this situation? and why?"
- Try new activities, hobbies, or subjects that interest you. Exploring different areas can help you discover what you're passionate about and what brings you joy.
- Sometimes, friends and family can offer valuable perspectives on your strengths and qualities. While it's important to trust your own judgment. Listening to the feedback of those who know you well can provide additional insights.
- Practices like meditation and mindfulness can help you tune into your inner self and become more aware of your thoughts and feelings. This awareness is crucial for understanding who you are and what you want.

BUILDING RESILIENCE THROUGH SELF-LOVE

Resilience is the capacity to return from mishaps and face challenges with a positive outlook. It's an essential quality to create as you explore the ups and downs of life. Self-love plays a significant part in building resilience, as it gives the foundation of strength for self-worth and certainty. At the point when you love yourself, you're bound to move toward challenges with a feeling of idealism and assurance. You comprehend that difficulties are a characteristic piece of life and that they don't characterize your value. Rather than being deterred by challenges, you view them as any open doors for development and learning. You start following the below techniques and see the changes within your inner self.

- Embrace challenges as opportunities to learn and grow. Understand that your abilities and intelligence can be developed through effort and persistence.
- Be kind to yourself when things don't go as planned. Treat yourself with the same compassion and understanding that you would offer to a friend in a similar situation.
- Set achievable goals that align with your values and interests. Break larger goals into smaller ones. manageable steps to maintain motivation and build confidence.
- Surround yourself with people who uplift and support you. Having a strong support network can provide encouragement and perspective during challenging times.
- Strengthen your ability to address and resolve problems by practicing critical thinking and creative problem-solving techniques. This will enhance your confidence in handling difficult situations.

THE RIPPLE EFFECT OF SELF-LOVE

One of the most gorgeous parts of self-love is its far reaching influence on individuals around you. At the point when you love and respect yourself, it decidedly impacts your associations with others. You become a good example for self-care and self-respect, rousing others to treat themselves with a similar benevolence and compassion. Your self-love can likewise add to a more certain and strong community. At the point when you practice self-love, you're bound to participate in certain events, make sound connections and to help others in their journeys. This makes a gradually expanding influence, where your activities motivate others to embrace self-love and strengthen, prompting a more compassionate and connected community. The impact of self-love extends beyond your immediate community — it can possibly impact people in the future. By developing self-love, you're assisting with breaking patterns of cynicism and self-question that can be gone down through families and social orders. At the point when you model self-love and self-respect, you're showing the cutting edge that they, as well, deserve love and consideration. As you proceed with your journey, consider how your activities could impact others, particularly more youthful individuals who admire you. Your obligation to self-love can move them to leave on their own journeys, making a tradition of strengthening and positive change. In reality as we know it, where self-analysis and pessimism are in many cases the standard. Picking self-love is a strong demonstration of obstruction. It's tied in with making a culture of strengthening, where individuals are urged to embrace their uniqueness, praise their assets, and back each other's development. By practicing self-love, you're contributing to this culture of empowerment. You're helping to create a world where people are valued for who they are. rather than for what they achieve or how they look. This culture shift starts with individuals like you who are willing to challenge the status quo and prioritize self-love in their lives.

Real Life Stories Of Self-Love

EMMA'S JOURNEY TO SELF-LOVE

Emma was a high-achieving student who always prided herself on her academic accomplishments. Nonetheless. underneath her prosperity was a well established feeling of dread toward disappointment and a steady requirement for approval from others. Emma's self-worth was attached to her grades, and any mishap felt like an individual disappointment. Over the long haul, Emma understood that her quest for flawlessness was negatively affecting her psychological and close to home prosperity. She was continually worried, restless, and depleted.

At some point, after a particularly difficult semester. Emma chose to make a stride back and reexamine her relationship with herself. Emma began practicing self-compassion, reminding herself that her worth wasn't determined by her grades or achievements. She started journaling, reflecting on her thoughts and feelings, and challenging her negative self-talk. She also set boundaries with her studies, allowing herself time to rest and recharge. As Emma's self-love developed, she saw a change in her viewpoint. She was not generally characterized by her achievements, and she felt more sure about her capacity to explore life's challenges. Emma's journey to self-love instructed her that she was sufficient, similarly as she was. and that she had the right to treat herself with graciousness and respect.

MIA'S EMBRACE OF HER BODY

Mia battled with self-perception issues for a large portion of her young years. She frequently contrasted herself with others and felt deficient in light of the fact that she didn't fit society's principles of magnificence. Mia's self-regard was profoundly impacted, and she frequently participated in negative self-talk about her appearance. Following quite a while of battling. Mia chose to leave on a journey of self-love. She began by testing her negative self-talk and supplanting it with positive affirmations. Mia likewise started following body-positive powerhouses via virtual entertainment, who urged her to embrace her body as it was. Mia made a conscious effort to stop comparing herself to others and instead focused on celebrating her unique beauty. She started practicing self-care, nourishing her body with healthy foods, and engaging in physical activities that made her feel strong and empowered. As Mia's self-love grew, she began to see her body in a new light. She no longer felt the need to conform to societal standards, and she embraced her body for all that it was. Mia's journey to self-love taught her that true beauty comes from within and that she deserved to love and care for herself. just as she was.

SARAH'S PATH TO SELF-ACCEPTANCE

Sarah was an accommodating person who frequently put others' requirements before her own. She battled with defining limits and frequently discovered herself feeling overpowered and depleted. Sarah's self-worth was attached to others' endorsement, and she expected that defining limits would prompt dismissal.

In the wake of encountering burnout. Sarah understood that she expected to roll out an improvement. She started by considering her qualities and needs, perceiving that her prosperity expected to start things out. Sarah began rehearsing self-love by defining solid limits and figuring out how to say no when necessary. Sarah additionally searched out steady connections and moved away from the individuals who exploited her generosity. She rehearsed self-compassion, advising herself that it was OK to focus on her necessities and that she should have been treated with deference. As Sarah's self-love developed, she turned out to be more certain about her capacity to define limits and defend herself. She as of now did not want to look for others' endorsement, and she embraced her value as a person. Sarah's journey to self-love showed her-self-respect is a fundamental part of a sound and satisfying life.

Overcoming Common Challenges In The Self-Love Journey

"Facing Self-Doubt"- Self-doubt is perhaps one of the most widely recognized challenges individuals face on their self-love journey. That little voice in your mind questions your value, your capacities, and your true capacity. While self-doubt is a characteristic piece of being human, it can turn into a huge obstruction in the event that it's not tended to. Overcoming self-doubt requires a combination of self-awareness and self-compassion. First, you need to recognize when self-doubt is creeping in. Pay attention to your thoughts and notice when you're being overly critical or harsh with yourself. Once you've identified these thoughts. challenge them with more positivity, realistic beliefs. Remind yourself of your strengths and accomplishments, and practice being kind to yourself, especially when you're struggling.

DEALING WITH EXTERNAL PRESSURES

In this day and age, outer tensions can make it hard to keep areas of strength for self-love. Whether it's cultural assumptions, peer pressure. or the impact of online entertainment. These outside variables can cause you to question your value or to feel like you're not adequate. The way to managing outer tensions is to remain grounded in your qualities and your sense of identity. Advise yourself that you're not set in stone by outside factors like appearance, fame, or accomplishments. Center around the main thing to you, and settle on decisions that line up with your qualities instead of attempting to meet another person's assumptions.

NAVIGATING NEGATIVE RELATIONSHIPS

Relationships are a fundamental piece of life, however not all connections are positive or steady. In some cases, individuals around you — whether companions. Relatives, or love partners — can be a wellspring of pessimism or toxicity. Exploring negative connections requires boldness and self-respect. Assuming somebody in your life is reliably causing you to really regret yourself or subverting your self-worth, it may be necessary to set boundaries or even distance yourself from that relationship. Keep in mind, you should be encircled by individuals who elevate and uphold you, not the people who cut you down.

HANDLING SETBACKS

Setbacks are inevitable on any journey, and the self-love journey is no exemption. There will be times when you battle, when old propensities reemerge, or when you feel like you're not gaining ground. It's essential to comprehend that difficulties as a natural piece of development and that they don't characterize your value or your journey. At the point when you experience difficulty, attempt to move toward it with interest as opposed to judgment. Ask yourself what you can gain from the experience and how you can utilize it to push ahead. Keep in mind, self-love isn't tied in with being awesome, it's tied in with being caring to yourself and proceeding to develop, even despite challenges.

CONCLUSION ON EMBRACING THE MYSTIQUE OF YOUR INNER BEAUTY

Discovering the mystique of your inner beauty is a transformative journey that requires patience, compassion, and a commitment to self-love. It's about recognizing your worth, embracing your uniqueness, and treating yourself with the kindness and respect you deserve. Remember, self-love is not a destination. It's a lifelong journey. There will be ups and downs, but each step you take toward loving yourself is a step toward a more fulfilling and authentic life. Embrace the journey, celebrate your progress, and continue to nurture the relationship you have with yourself. As you move forward, keep these words close to your heart: You are worthy of love, just as you are. You are enough, just as you are, and you deserve to live a life that is true to who you are. Now, take a deep breath. give yourself a warm hug, and let's continue this journey together. The next chapter is all about developing a positive self-image—a crucial aspect of self-love that will empower you to shine your light even brighter.

Chapter 2

Developing A Positive Self-Image

Recognizing Your Strengths and Talents

Fostering a positive self-image begins with perceiving your assets and talents. It's not difficult to focus on your apparent shortcomings or the things you want to change about yourself, however this attitude can lead to self-doubt and negative self-discernment. To develop a positive self-image, you should move your concentration to your unique qualities — the qualities and talents that make you what you are. Perceiving your strengths is critical in light of the fact that it helps construct self-certainty. At the point when you're mindful of what you're great at, you're bound to move toward challenges with a feeling of capacity and confirmation. It likewise assists you with pursuing choices that line up with your capacities, prompting a seriously satisfying and fruitful life. However, perceiving your strengths isn't just about boosting your confidence. It's likewise about figuring out yourself on a more profound level. It's about appreciating the qualities that set you apart and acknowledging the contributions you can make to the world. When you recognize your strengths, you begin to see yourself as a valuable and capable individual, which is a key component of a positive self-image.

HOW TO IDENTIFY YOUR STRENGTHS?

Identifying your strengths can sometimes be challenging, especially if you're used to downplaying your abilities or comparing yourself to others. Here are some strategies to help you recognize and embrace your strengths:

- Think about the times in your life when you've felt proud of yourself or when you've achieved something significant. What skills or qualities did you use to accomplish those things? Reflecting on your past successes can help you identify the strengths that have helped you along the way.

- Sometimes, It's easier for others to see our strengths than it is for us to see them ourselves. Ask trusted friends, family members, or mentors for feedback on what they think your strengths are. Their insights can provide valuable perspective and help you see yourself in a more positive light.

- There are many strengths assessments available online that can help you identify your core strengths. These assessments typically ask you to answer questions about your preferences, behaviors, and attitudes, and then provide you with a list of strengths based on your responses. Some popular assessments include the VIA Character Strengths Survey and the CliftonStrengths assessment.

- The things you enjoy doing are often linked to your strengths. When you're engaged in activities that you're good at, you're more likely to experience a sense of flow and satisfaction. Take note of the activities that bring you joy and fulfillment—these can be clues to your strengths.

- How you respond to challenges can reveal a lot about your strengths. Do you stay calm under pressure? Are you good at problem-solving? Do you persevere when things get tough? Observing your behavior in challenging situations can help you identify the strengths that you rely on in difficult times.

EMBRACING YOUR STRENGTHS

Once you've identified your strengths. The next step is to embrace them. This means acknowledging your strengths with pride and using them to your advantage. It's about giving yourself permission to shine and recognizing that your strengths are an important part of who you are. Find an opportunity to praise your strengths and the positive effect they have on your life. Whether it's writing them down in a diary, imparting them to a companion, or essentially pausing for a minute to see the value in them, praising your strengths supports your positive self-image and assists you with building certainty. While laying out objectives, consider how your strengths can assist you with accomplishing them. Adjusting your objectives to your strengths builds your odds of coming out on top and permits you to use your novel capacities. For instance, assuming one of your strengths is innovativeness, put forth objectives that permit you to communicate and foster your imaginative talents. Make it a point to impart your strengths to other people. Whether it's in an individual or expert setting, utilizing your strengths to help other people benefits them as well as supports your own feeling of significant worth and capacity. It's a way of contributing to the world in a meaningful way. Affirm your strengths regularly by reminding yourself of what you're good at. Positive affirmations can be a powerful tool for reinforcing a positive self-image. For example, you might say to yourself, "I am a strong and capable individual." or "I have unique talents that make me valuable."

OVERCOMING THE FEAR OF EMBRACING YOUR STRENGTHS

As far as some might be concerned. Embracing their strengths can scare. You could stress that recognizing your strengths will seem to be egotistical or proud. In any case, there's a contrast between self-certainty and presumption. Self-certainty is tied in with perceiving your value and capacities without decreasing the value of others, while pomposity includes an expanded identity significance. It's essential that embracing your strengths doesn't mean you're ignoring your shortcomings. It just implies that you're deciding to focus on the positive parts of yourself, which is fundamental for fostering a positive self-image. Everybody has strengths and shortcomings, and recognizing your strengths is a sound and fundamental piece of self-development.

- Identifying One's Personal Strengths – Building on the previous section, identifying your personal strengths is a critical step in developing a positive self-image. Personal strengths are the attributes, skills, and qualities that come naturally to you and that you excel in. These can be intellectual strengths related to your ability to think critically, solve problems, and acquire knowledge. Examples include analytical thinking, creativity, curiosity, and a love of learning. Emotional strengths pertain to your ability to manage and understand your emotions and the emotions of others. Examples include empathy, emotional intelligence, resilience, and self-awareness. Social strengths are related to your ability to interact effectively with others. Examples include communication skills, leadership, teamwork, and the ability to build strong relationships. Physical strengths involve your physical abilities and how you use your body. Examples include athleticism, coordination, endurance, and physical fitness. Character strengths are virtues or qualities that define who you are as a person. Examples include integrity, honesty, kindness, and a strong work ethic.
- Ways To Identify Your Strengths - Look back on your life experiences and consider the minutes when you felt glad for yourself or when others perceived your accomplishments. What characteristics or abilities did you use in those minutes? Considering your encounters can assist you with recognizing the strengths

that played a huge impact in your life. Contemplate the exercises or undertakings that fall into place for you or that you view as simple to do. These could be signs of your own strengths. For instance, on the off chance that you find it simple to associate with others and fabricate connections, social strengths like compassion and correspondence might be among your strengths. As referenced before, asking others for input can be a significant method for distinguishing your own strengths. Individuals who know you well, like friends, relatives, or associates, can give experiences into the strengths they find in you. Strength's assessments, such as the VIA Character Strengths Survey or the Clifton Strengths assessment, can provide a structured approach to identifying your personal strengths. These evaluations are intended to assist you with finding your core strengths and comprehend how to utilize them for your potential benefit.

- How you handle challenges can reveal a lot about your personal strengths. Do you stay calm under pressure? Are you good at finding creative solutions to problems? Do you persevere when faced with obstacles? Observing your reactions to challenges can help you identify the strengths that you rely on in difficult situations. Once you've identified your personal strengths. The next step is to embrace and cultivate them. This involves acknowledging your strengths with pride and finding ways to develop and use them in your daily life. Take a moment to acknowledge and appreciate your personal strengths. Recognize that these strengths are an important part of who you are and that they contribute to your unique identity. Align your goals with your personal strengths. For example, if one of your strengths is creativity, set goals that allow you to express and develop your creative talents. Using your strengths to achieve your goals can increase your chances of success and lead to a more fulfilling life. Personal strengths are like muscles—the more you use and develop them, the stronger they become. Look for opportunities to build on your strengths, whether through education. practice, or new experiences. Use your personal strengths to make a positive impact on others. Whether it's helping a friend in need, volunteering, or simply being there for someone, sharing your strengths with others can reinforce your positive self-image and contribute to your sense of purpose.

Embracing Success

Success is a complex idea that can mean various things to various individuals. For some, success may be accomplishing a particular profession objective, while for other people. It may very well be self-awareness or having a constructive outcome on the world. Notwithstanding the way that you characterize success, embracing your successes is a fundamental piece of fostering a positive self-image. Before you can embrace success, it's important to understand what success means to you. Success is not a one-size-fits-all concept—it's deeply personal and can vary based on your values, goals, and aspirations. To define success for yourself, consider the following questions:

- What are your personal and professional goals?
- What values are most important to you?
- What achievements or milestones make you feel proud?
- How do you measure success in your life?

By reflecting on these questions, you can gain clarity on what success means to you and how it aligns with your overall vision for your life. Embracing success is significant on the grounds that it builds up your positive self-image and lifts your self-certainty. At the point when you recognize and praise your successes, you're insisting on your capacities and perceiving the work and assurance it took to accomplish your objectives. Nonetheless, embracing success isn't just about commending the huge successes — it's additionally about perceiving the more modest, regular successes that add to your general development and prosperity. Whether it's finishing a difficult project at work, conquering an individual impediment, or essentially moving toward a better way of life, each success regardless of how little, should be recognized.

CONQUERING HARDSHIPS IN EMBRACING SUCCESS

For some, embracing success can be challenging. You might struggle with self-doubt, fear of judgment, or the belief that you're not worthy of success. These barriers can prevent you from fully recognizing and celebrating your achievements. Here are some common barriers to embracing success and how to overcome them:

- Imposter Syndrome – An inability to acknowledge success is the inclination that you're not so able or competent as others see you to be. You could credit your successes to karma or outer elements, instead of your own abilities and capacities. To conquer an inability to acknowledge success, help yourself to remember your diligent effort, commitment, and the abilities you've created over the long haul. Track your accomplishments and allude to it while you're feeling self-doubt. Recollect that you've procured your success through your endeavors, and you have the right to celebrate it.

- Apprehension About Judgment – You might fear that others will judge you for celebrating your success, thinking that you're boastful or arrogant. This dread can keep you from completely embracing your accomplishments. To beat the apprehension about judgment, focus on your own bliss and prosperity. Recall that your success is an impression of your persistent effort and commitment, and you reserve each privilege to celebrate it. Encircle yourself with strong individuals who support and elevate you, and let go of the anxiety toward what others could think.

- Perfectionism – Perfectionism is the conviction that you should accomplish faultless outcomes in all that you do. If you're a perfectionist, you might downplay your successes because you feel they're not "perfect" enough. To conquer perfectionism, practice self-compassion and perceive that nobody is great. Commend your advancement and the work you've placed into your accomplishments, regardless of whether the result isn't precisely as you imagined. Recollect that success is about development and learning, not tied in with being great.

Once you've overcome the barriers to embracing success. It's time to start celebrating your achievements. Take time to celebrate your successes, both big and small. Whether it's treating yourself to something special, sharing your achievements with loved ones, or simply taking a moment to reflect on your accomplishments, celebrating your wins reinforces your positive self-image and boosts your confidence. Success is often the result of a long and challenging journey. Reflect on the steps you took to achieve your goals. the obstacles you overcame, and the lessons you learned along the way. Acknowledging the effort and determination it took to succeed can help you appreciate your achievements even more. Sharing your success with others can be a powerful way to celebrate your achievements and inspire those around you. Whether it's sharing your story on social media, giving a speech, or simply telling a friend, sharing your success can create a ripple effect of positivity and encouragement. Practicing gratitude is a powerful way to embrace success. Take time to express gratitude for the opportunities, resources, and support that helped you achieve your goals. Gratitude not only enhances your positive self-image but also fosters a sense of contentment and fulfillment. Embracing success doesn't mean resting on your laurels. Once you've celebrated your achievements, set new goals that challenge you to continue growing and evolving. Setting new goals keeps you motivated and focused on your personal and professional development.

DEFEATING NEGATIVE SELF-TALK

Negative self-talk is the internal dialogue that criticizes, doubts, and undermines your self-worth. It's that little voice in your head that tells you you're not good enough, that you'll never succeed, or that you're unworthy of love and happiness. Negative self-talk can be incredibly damaging to your self-image, leading to low self-esteem, anxiety, and even depression. Negative self-talk often stems from a combination of past experiences, societal pressures, and deeply ingrained beliefs about yourself. It can appear in different structures, including:

- Personalizing - Faulting yourself for things that turn out badly, in any event, when it's not your fault.
- Catastrophizing - Anticipating the absolute worst result in any circumstance.
- Filtering - Focusing just on the negative parts of a circumstance while disregarding the up-sides.
- Highly contrasting Thinking - Seeing things in extremes. with no middle ground (e.g ... "I'm either a total success or a complete disappointment").
- Strategies for Overcoming Negative Self-Talk - Overcoming negative self-talk is essential for developing a positive self-image. Here are some strategies to help you silence your inner critic and replace negative thoughts with positive. empowering ones:
- The most vital phase in conquering negative self-talk is to become mindful of it. Focus on the considerations that go through your head over the course of the day, particularly in circumstances where you feel worried, restless, or self-critical. Notice the examples in your reasoning and recognize the negative considerations that are generally common.
- Whenever you've distinguished your negative considerations. Now is the right time to challenge them. Find out if these contemplations depend on realities or presumptions. Is it safe to say that they are level headed, or would they say they are overstated and ridiculous? By testing your negative considerations, you can begin to perceive the truth about them — pointless and unwarranted.
- Positive affirmations are explanations that build up your self-worth and help you to remember your strengths. At the point when you discover yourself participating in negative self-talk, supplant those contemplations with positive assertions. For instance, assuming you wind up thinking, "I'm not sufficient." supplant it with, "I am capable and deserving of success."
- Self-compassion includes treating yourself with the very benevolence and understanding that you would propose to a companion. At the point when you commit an error or face a difficulty, rather than upbraiding yourself, practice self-compassion by recognizing your sentiments and advising yourself that being imperfect is OK. Self-compassion can help you break free from the cycle of negative self-talk and build a more positive self-image.
- Re-examining includes checking out at a circumstance according to an alternate point of view. Rather than focusing on the negative angles, attempt to see the up-sides or the examples you can gain from the experience. For instance, on the off chance that you didn't land the position you needed, rather than thinking, "I'm a disappointment." rethink your contemplations too, "This is a chance for

me to learn and develop, and there will be different open doors later on."

- The people you surround yourself with can fundamentally affect your self-talk. Invest energy with individuals who elevate and uphold you, and move away from the people who cut you down or build up negative reasoning. Positive impacts can assist you with fostering a more sure self-image and build up your endeavors to beat negative self-talk.
- Mindfulness includes being available at the time and noticing your contemplations and sentiments without judgment. By practicing mindfulness, you can turn out to be more mindful of your negative self-talk and figure out how to relinquish it, as opposed to becoming involved with it. Mindfulness techniques like reflection, profound breathing, and establishing activities can assist you with remaining fixated and focused on the current second.

Negative self-talk can be a powerful force, shaping your perceptions of yourself and the world around you. It can create a self-fulfilling prophecy, where your negative thoughts lead to negative outcomes, reinforcing your belief that you're not good enough. Negative self-talk can significantly affect your self-image. At the point when you continually criticize and put down yourself, you begin to accept that the negative things you're saying are valid. This can prompt an endless loop of self-doubt, low self-respect, and a negative self-image. Over the long run, negative self-talk can dissolve your confidence, making it challenging to seek your goals or face challenges. It can likewise influence your connections, as you might battle to trust that you genuinely deserve love and respect. In some cases, negative self-talk might add to psychological wellness issues like tension and depression.

THE POWER OF POSITIVE SELF-TALK

Positive self-talk is the antidote to negative self-talk. It involves replacing negative thoughts with positive, empowering ones that reinforce your self-worth and build your confidence. Positive self-talk can help you develop a more positive self-image, improve your mental health, and achieve your goals. Always say-
"I am capable and competent."
"I am deserving of love and respect."
"I am proud of my accomplishments."
"I can handle whatever challenges come my way."
"I am worthy of success and happiness."
Incorporating positive self-talk into your daily routine can have a profound impact on your self-image and overall well-being. It's a practice that requires consistency and effort. but the rewards are well worth it.

TRANSFORMATIVE POWER OF SELF-LOVE

Transformation is at the heart of the self-love journey. It's about moving from a place of self-doubt and insecurity to a space where you fully embrace and celebrate who you are. This process of transformation isn't always easy—it involves shedding old beliefs, habits, and thought patterns that no longer serve you and replacing them with healthier ones, more empowering ones. Self-love is the catalyst for this transformation. When you begin to truly love and accept yourself, you start to see the world differently. You become more confident, more resilient, and more capable of facing life's challenges. The transformation isn't just about changing how you see yourself. It's about changing how you engage with the world around you. Stages of Personal Transformation:
- The first step in any transformation is awareness.

You need to recognize the areas of your life where you're not being true to yourself or where you're holding onto negative beliefs. This might involve reflecting on your relationships, your self-talk, or the choices you've been making.
- Once you're aware of the areas that need change. The next step is acceptance. This means acknowledging where you are without judgment and understanding that it's okay to be a work in progress. Acceptance is about loving yourself as you are while also being open to growth and change.
- Transformation requires action. This means taking concrete steps to change the patterns and behaviors that are holding you back. It might involve setting new goals, changing your habits, or practicing new ways of thinking. The key is to be consistent, intentional action that aligns with your vision of who you want to be.
- The final stage of transformation is sustaining the change. This means making self-love a daily practice and continuing to grow and evolve. It's about staying committed to your journey, even when it's challenging, and continuously working to improve yourself.
- As you transform, you'll start to notice changes in how you feel and how you interact with the world. You might find that you're more confident, more compassionate, and more at peace with yourself. You might also notice that your relationships improve, and that you're more successful in pursuing your goals. It's important to embrace these changes and celebrate your growth. Transformation isn't about becoming someone else—it's about becoming more of who you truly are. As you continue to grow and evolve, remember to honor the journey you've been on and to appreciate the person you're becoming.

SELF-LOVE AS A DAILY PRACTICE

One of the keys to cultivating self-love is consistency. Just like any other important aspect of life, self-love requires regular attention and effort. It's not something you can practice once and then forget about. It's a daily commitment to yourself and your well-being. Making self-love a daily practice means integrating it into every aspect of your life. It's about being mindful of how you talk to yourself, how you treat your body, and how you engage with others. It's about making choices that reflect your worth and your values, even when it's difficult. Follow these practices daily:

- Start your day with intention by setting aside time each morning for self-care. This could be a few minutes of meditation, journaling, or simply reflecting on what you're grateful for. Starting your day with positive intentions sets the tone for the rest of the day.
- Incorporate positive affirmations into your daily routine. These are simple. powerful statements that reinforce your self-worth and encourage a positive mindset. For example, you might say, "I am worthy of love and respect." or "I am capable of achieving my goals."
- Practice setting and maintaining healthy boundaries throughout your day. This might involve saying no to requests that drain your energy or taking time for yourself when you need it. Boundaries are essential for protecting your well-being and ensuring that your needs are met.
- Self-love includes taking care of your physical health. Make choices that nourish your body, whether that's eating nutritious foods, staying hydrated, getting enough sleep, or engaging in regular physical activity. Treat your body with the care and respect it deserves.

- At the end of each day, take a few moments to reflect on your experiences and what you've learned. Practice gratitude by acknowledging the positive aspects of your day and the progress you've made. Reflection helps reinforce the positive changes you're making and keeps you focused on your journey.

Self-love isn't just a practice. It's a way of life. It's about making choices that align with your values and treating yourself with the kindness and respect you deserve. As you integrate self-love into your daily routine, you'll start to notice how it influences every aspect of your life—from your relationships to your work to your overall sense of happiness and fulfillment.

Building Confidence Through Positive Reinforcement

Building confidence is an ongoing process that involves reinforcing your positive qualities, achievements, and efforts. Positive reinforcement is a powerful tool that can help you build confidence and develop a positive self-image.

WHAT IS POSITIVE REINFORCEMENT?

Positive reinforcement includes remunerating yourself for your achievements, endeavors, and positive ways of behaving. It's tied in with recognizing and praising your successes, regardless of how little, and utilizing those successes to construct your confidence and self-respect. Positive reinforcement can take many structures. including:

- Finding an opportunity to commend your accomplishments, whether it's indulging yourself with something uniquely great, imparting your success to other people, or just pausing for a minute to consider your achievements. Celebrating your successes and rewarding yourself for your efforts can boost your confidence and reinforce your belief in your abilities.

- Building up your self-worth and abilities through positive certifications that help you to remember your strengths and accomplishments. Positive reinforcement helps you build a positive self-image by focusing on your strengths and achievements, rather than your perceived shortcomings.
- Giving yourself a reward for achieving a goal or completing a challenging task. This could be something tangible, like a gift, or something intangible, like taking time for self-care. When you reward yourself for achieving your goals, you're more likely to stay motivated and continue working toward your aspirations. Positive reinforcement can improve your overall well-being by reducing stress, increasing happiness, and promoting a sense of fulfillment.

INCORPORATING POSITIVE REINFORCEMENT INTO YOUR LIFE

Start by setting achievable goals that align with your strengths and values. When you achieve these goals, take time to celebrate your success and reward yourself for your efforts. Incorporate positive affirmations into your daily routine. These affirmations can reinforce your self-worth and remind you of your capabilities. Repeat them to yourself in the morning, throughout the day, and before bed. Take time to celebrate your successes, both big and small. Whether it's completing a challenging project, reaching a personal milestone, or simply making progress toward a goal, celebrate your wins and acknowledge the effort it took to achieve them. Reward yourself for your accomplishments. This could be something tangible, like treating yourself to a special meal or buying something you've been wanting, or something intangible. like taking a day off to relax and recharge. Be kind to yourself and practice self-compassion, especially when you face challenges or setbacks. Acknowledge your efforts and remind yourself that it's okay to be imperfect. Self-compassion is a form of positive reinforcement that can help you build resilience and confidence. Surround yourself with people who uplift and support you. Positive influences can reinforce your efforts to build confidence and develop a positive self-image. Seek out relationships with people who celebrate your successes and encourage you to reach your goals.

CONCLUSION TO THIS CHAPTER

Developing a positive self-image is a journey that involves recognizing and embracing your strengths, overcoming negative self-talk, and building confidence through positive reinforcement. It's about shifting your focus from your perceived shortcomings to your unique qualities and achievements. By incorporating the strategies outlined in this chapter into your daily routine, you can cultivate a positive self-image that empowers you to live a fulfilling and successful life. Remember, developing a positive self-image is an ongoing process that requires patience, self-compassion, and a commitment to personal growth. Celebrate your progress, embrace your successes, and continue to nurture your self-worth every day.

Chapter 3

Embracing Your Inner Power

What Does It Mean To Be Empowered?

Empowerment is a profound and transformative concept, one that goes beyond mere surface-level confidence. At its core, to be empowered means to recognize and embrace the inherent strength that resides within you. It's about understanding that you have the power to shape your own life, to make decisions that reflect your true self, and to stand firm in your beliefs and values, even in the face of adversity. Empowerment is not something that happens overnight. It's a journey of self-discovery, self-acceptance, and self-love. It involves peeling back the layers of doubt, fear, and insecurity that may have built up over time, and reconnecting with the essence of who you are. This process allows you to reclaim your personal power and use it to create the life you truly desire. One of the most important aspects of empowerment is realizing that you are the author of your own story. You have the ability to choose your path, to decide what is important to you, and to pursue your goals with determination and confidence. Empowerment also means understanding that while you cannot control everything that happens in life, you can control how you respond to it. This perspective shift can be incredibly liberating, as it allows you to focus on what you can influence, rather than getting bogged down by what you cannot.

Empowerment is deeply connected to self-love and self-respect. When you love and respect yourself, you naturally begin to make choices that are in alignment with your well-being. You start to prioritize your needs, set boundaries, and refuse to settle for less than you deserve. This. in turn, builds your confidence and reinforces your sense of self-worth, creating a positive cycle of empowerment. Empowerment is also about embracing your uniqueness. Each of us has our own set of strengths, talents, and qualities that make us who we are. When you recognize and celebrate these aspects of yourself, you unlock a deep well of inner power that can propel you forward in life. This power is not about dominating others or being the best in a competitive sense. It's about being the best version of yourself and living a life that is true to you. In summary, to be empowered is to live authentically, to embrace your inner strength, and to stand confidently in your truth. It's about taking control of your life, making choices that honor your values, and believing in your ability to achieve your goals. Your body is a beautiful part of who you are, no matter what shape, size, or color it is. Understanding that body image is more than just what we see in the mirror is the first step toward self-love. It's about how you feel in your own skin and how you treat your body with kindness and respect.

DISCOVERING YOUR INNER STRENGTH

Discovering your inner strength is a journey that requires self-reflection, trustworthiness, and mental fortitude. It's tied in with glimpsing inside and perceiving the versatility, assurance, and power that you as of now have. regardless of whether you haven't completely taken advantage of it yet. Inner strength isn't tied in with being strong or never feeling dread or uncertainty, it's tied in with realizing that you have the ability to defeat difficulties, regardless of how troublesome they might appear. Quite possibly the earliest move toward discovering your inner strength is to recognize your previous encounters and how they have formed you. Contemplate the difficulties you've looked at in your life — large or little — and how you figured out how to get past them. Maybe you didn't understand it at that point. Yet those minutes required strength, flexibility, and persistence. Reflecting on these experiences can help you see just how strong you really are. Inner strength is also closely tied to self-belief. It's the confidence that you can handle whatever comes your way, even if you don't have all the answers right now. This belief in yourself is not something that comes naturally to everyone, especially if you've faced criticism or doubt from others. However, building self-belief is possible, and it starts with challenging the negative thoughts and self-doubt that may be holding you back. One more key part of inner strength is emotional resilience. Life is loaded with ups and downs, and being sincerely versatile means having the option to return from mishaps, adjust to change, and continue to push ahead, in any event, when things are extreme. Profound flexibility doesn't mean smothering your sentiments or imagining all is great when it's not. Rather, It's about allowing yourself to feel your emotions. process them, and then find the strength to keep going. Discovering your inner strength additionally includes perceiving your qualities and what makes the biggest difference to you. At the point when you are sure about your qualities, you are better prepared to pursue choices that line up with what your identity is and a big motivator for you. This clarity gives you the strength to say no to things that don't serve you and to pursue the things that do, even when it's difficult. It's important to remember that inner strength is not a finite resource, it grows and develops the more you use it. Every time you face a challenge, take a risk, or step out of your comfort zone, you are building your inner strength. The more you trust in your ability to handle life's challenges, the stronger you become.

UNDERSTANDING WHAT PERSONAL EM-POWERMENT TRULY IS

Personal empowerment is a powerful state of being where you fully recognize and embrace your ability to make decisions, take action, and shape your life according to your desires and values. It's about understanding that you are in control of your destiny, and that you have the power to create the life you want, regardless of external circumstances. At the heart of personal empowerment is self-awareness. To be truly empowered, you must first know yourself—your strengths, weaknesses, values, and beliefs. This self-awareness allows you to make decisions that are in alignment with who you are and what you want out of life. It also enables you to recognize when something is not serving you, so you can make the necessary changes to move forward. Another key component of personal empowerment is self-efficacy, which is the belief in your ability to achieve your goals and handle the challenges that come your way. This belief is not about being arrogant or overconfident, rather It's about having a realistic and positive view of your capabilities. When you believe in yourself, you are more likely to take action, even when the outcome is uncertain. This willingness to act is a hallmark of empowered individuals. Personal empowerment also involves taking responsibility for your life. This means owning your choices, actions, and outcomes. rather than blaming others or external factors for your circumstances. While it's true that we all face challenges and obstacles that are beyond our control, empowered individuals focus on what they can control—their thoughts, attitudes, and actions. This shift in focus can be incredibly liberating, as it allows you to reclaim your power and take charge of your life. Another important aspect of personal empowerment is setting and enforcing boundaries. Empowered individuals know their worth and are not afraid to set limits on what they will tolerate from others. They understand that boundaries are essential for maintaining their well-being and protecting their energy. By setting boundaries, you are not only taking care of yourself, but you are also teaching others how to treat you. Finally, Personal empowerment is about continuous growth and learning. Empowered individuals are always seeking to improve themselves, whether through learning new skills, gaining new knowledge, or challenging themselves in new ways. They understand that personal growth is a lifelong journey, and they are committed to becoming the best version of themselves. In short, Personal empowerment is about knowing yourself, believing in yourself, taking responsibility for your life, setting boundaries, and committing to continuous growth. It's about recognizing that you have the power within you to create the life you desire, and taking the necessary steps to make that life a reality.

Unlocking Your Potential

Unlocking your potential is tied in with taking advantage of the vast reserves of ability, imagination, and capacity that exists in you. It's tied in with perceiving that you are equipped for definitely more than you might understand, and allowing yourself to seek after your fantasies and aspirations without holding back. Perhaps the earliest move toward unlocking your potential is to relinquish restricting convictions. These are the negative considerations and suspicions that tell you're not good enough, smart enough, or capable enough to accomplish your objectives. Restricting convictions frequently come from previous encounters, cultural assumptions,

or the assessments of others. However, These beliefs are not truths—they are simply thoughts that you have the power to change. To open your potential. It's essential to challenge these restricting convictions and supplant them with empowering ones.

Begin by distinguishing the negative contemplations that are keeping you down. For instance, assuming you wind up thinking, "I could never do that," I wonder why not? What proof do you need to help this conviction? As a general rule, you'll observe that these convictions depend on dread instead of reality. Whenever you've recognized your restricting beliefs, work on supplanting them with positive affirmations. Affirmations are positive articulations that support your confidence in yourself and your capacities. For instance, rather than thinking, "I'm not adequate." you can share with yourself, "I'm skilled, and I have the ability to accomplish my objectives." over the long run. These affirmations will assist with revamping your reasoning and assembling your certainty. One more key part of unlocking your potential is putting forth ambitious goals. At the point when you put forth objectives that challenge you, you drive yourself to develop and foster in manners you never imagined. It's critical to define objectives that are significant to you and that line up with your qualities and interests.

At the point when you are pursuing something that genuinely makes a difference to you, you are bound to remain inspired and committed, in any event, whenever hard times arise. Unlocking your potential additionally requires getting out of your comfort zone. Development happens when you challenge yourself and face challenges. This could mean having a go at a new thing. taking on a challenging task, or placing yourself in a circumstance where you could fail. While getting out of your usual range of familiarity can be terrifying. It's additionally amazingly fulfilling. Each time you do, you prove to yourself that you are capable of more than you thought.

TAPPING INTO THE POWER WITHIN

The power within you is immense, and it is the key to living a fulfilling and purposeful life. This power is your inner strength, your intuition, and your ability to create the reality you desire. Tapping into this power is about connecting with your true self and using that connection to guide your actions and decisions. One of the most effective ways to tap into the power within is through mindfulness and self-reflection. Mindfulness is the practice of being present in the moment and paying attention to your thoughts, feelings, and sensations without judgment. When you are mindful, you become more aware of your inner world and the power that resides within you. Self-reflection is another powerful tool for tapping into your inner power. By taking the time to reflect on your experiences, thoughts, and emotions, you can gain a deeper understanding of yourself and your inner strengths. This understanding allows you to make decisions that are in alignment with your true self and to take actions that empower you. Another important aspect of tapping into your inner power is trusting your intuition. Your intuition is your inner knowing. the voice that guides you in the right direction, even when it doesn't make logical sense.

Trusting your intuition means listening to that voice and allowing it to guide your decisions. This requires letting go of doubt and fear and having faith in yourself and your abilities. Tapping into your inner power also involves embracing your uniqueness. Each of us has a unique combination of strengths, talents, and qualities that make us who we are. When you embrace your uniqueness, you unlock a deep well of inner power that can propel you forward in life. This power is not about being better than others. It's about being the best version of yourself. Another key aspect of tapping into your inner power is taking inspired action. Inspired action is action that is motivated by your inner guidance and aligned with your true self. When you take inspired action, you are not just going through the motions or doing what others expect of you, you are taking steps that are in alignment with your deepest desires and values. This type of action is powerful because it is fueled by your inner strength and authenticity.

EMBRACING YOUR UNIQUE QUALITIES

Your unique qualities are what make you who you are, and embracing them is a key part of personal empowerment. When you embrace your uniqueness, you are not only accepting yourself as you are, but you are also celebrating the things that make you different from others. This acceptance and celebration of your uniqueness is what gives you the confidence to stand out. to be authentic, and to live a life that is true to you. One of the first steps in embracing your unique qualities is to identify them. Take some time to think about the things that make you different from others. These could be your strengths. talents, personality traits, or even your quirks. Whatever they are, recognize that these qualities are what make you special and that they are a part of what makes you valuable. Once you have identified your unique qualities. It's important to embrace them fully. This means letting go of any negative thoughts or beliefs that you may have about these qualities. For example, you may have been told that you are too sensitive or too outspoken, and as a result, you may have tried to suppress these aspects of yourself. However, These qualities are a part of who you are. and they should be embraced rather than hidden. Embracing your unique qualities also involves being proud of who you are. This doesn't mean being arrogant or boastful. It simply means recognizing your value and not being afraid to show the world who you are. When you are proud of who you are. you radiate confidence and self-assurance, which in turn attracts positive opportunities and relationships into your life.

Another important aspect of embracing your unique qualities is using them to your advantage. Your unique qualities are your strengths, and when you use them in the right way. They can help you achieve your goals and live a fulfilling life. For example, if you are creative, use your creativity to solve problems and come up with innovative ideas. If you are empathetic. use your empathy to connect with others and build strong relationships. Embracing your unique qualities also involves being authentic. Authenticity is about being true to yourself and living in a way that is consistent with your values, beliefs, and desires. When you are authentic, you are not trying to be someone you're not, instead you are embracing who you are and expressing that to the world. This authenticity is what gives you the power to live a life that is true to you. It's easy to feel like you have to look a certain way to be valued or accepted. But remember, the images you see in the media are often edited and don't reflect real life. You are enough just as you are. Everybody is unique, and that's what makes each of us special. Instead of comparing yourself to others, celebrate what makes you, "YOU".

SETTING AND ACHIEVING GOALS

Setting and achieving goals is a powerful way to take control of your life and create the future you desire. Goals give you direction and purpose, and they provide a roadmap for achieving your dreams. When you set and achieve goals, you build confidence in your abilities and reinforce your sense of self-worth. One of the first steps in setting goals is to create a vision for your future. This vision is a clear and compelling picture of what you want your life to look like. It's about imagining your ideal life and thinking about the things that would make you truly happy and fulfilled. This vision should be based on your values, passions, and desires, and it should be something that excites and motivates you. Once you have a clear vision for your future. The next step is to have specific, measurable, achievable, relevant, and time-bound (SMART) goals that will help you achieve that vision. SMART goals are goals that are clearly defined and have a clear timeline for completion. They are also realistic and achievable, meaning that they are within your reach, given your current resources and capabilities. When setting SMART goals. It's important to be specific about what you want to achieve. For example, instead of setting a vague goal like "I want to be healthier." set a specific goal like "I want to exercise for 30 minutes a day, five days a week." This specificity gives you a clear target to aim for and makes it easier to track your progress. It's also important to make your goals measurable. This means setting goals that have a clear outcome that you can measure. For example, instead of setting a goal like "I want to save more money." set a measurable goal like "I want to save $500 by the end of the month." This measurability allows you to track your progress and know when you've achieved your goal.

Another important aspect of goal-setting is making sure your goals are achievable. This means setting goals that are within your reach, given your current resources and capabilities. While it's important to challenge yourself. It's also important to be realistic. Setting goals that are too ambitious can lead to frustration and disappointment if you don't achieve them. Your goals should also be relevant, meaning that they are aligned with your values, passions, and long-term vision for your life. When your goals are relevant, they are more likely to be meaningful and motivating, which increases your chances of achieving them. Finally, your goals should be time-bound, meaning that they have a clear deadline for completion. This deadline creates a sense of urgency and helps you stay focused and motivated, without a deadline. It's easy to procrastinate and put off working on your goals. Once you've set your SMART goals. The next step is to take action. This means breaking your goals down into smaller ones. manageable steps and taking consistent action towards achieving them. It's important to stay focused and motivated. even when things get tough. Remember, the road to achieving your goals is not always smooth, but if you stay committed and keep pushing forward, you will eventually achieve them. Take time each day to appreciate your body for what it does, not just how it looks. Your legs carry you, your arms embrace those you love, and your smile brightens someone's day. These are the things that truly matter. Try looking in the mirror and saying something kind to yourself. It might feel awkward at first, but with practice, it can become a powerful habit.

CREATING A VISION FOR YOUR FUTURE

Making a vision for your future is a strong method for assuming command over your life and shaping the way you need to follow. A vision is an unmistakable and convincing image of what you believe your life should resemble, and it fills in as an aide for the choices and moves you make en route. At the point when you have a vision for your future, you are bound to keep on track and persevere, even notwithstanding difficulties. Perhaps the earliest move toward making a vision for your future is to contemplate what you really truly desire. This requires self-reflection and honesty, as need might arise to be clear about your qualities, interests, and wants. Contemplate the things that satisfy you, the things that move you, and the things that you are energetic about. These are the building blocks of your vision. When you have an unmistakable comprehension of what you need. The following stage is to envision your optimal life. This is the everyday routine that you would experience assuming there were no restrictions or obstructions in your manner. Ponder where you would reside. what you would do for work, how you would invest your energy, and who you would encircle yourself with. This vision ought to be point by point and explicit, as the more unambiguous you are, the more clear your way will turn into. Likewise critical to contemplate the qualities will direct your vision. Your qualities are the standards and convictions that are generally vital to you, and they ought to be at the center of your vision. For example, if one of your values is kindness, then your vision should include ways to incorporate kindness into your daily life.

Another important aspect of creating a vision for your future is to think about the impact you want to have on the world. This is about thinking beyond yourself and considering how you can use your unique strengths and talents to make a positive difference in the lives of others. Whether it's through your work, your relationships, or your community. Your vision should include a sense of purpose and contribution. When you have a reasonable vision for your future. It's critical to record it on paper. Recording your vision assists with hardening it in your psyche and makes it more unmistakable. You can likewise make a vision board, which is a visual portrayal of your vision. This can incorporate pictures, words, and images that address your objectives and dreams. Keeping your vision board where you can see it consistently will act as a steady wake up call of what you are really going after. Finally, It's important to review and update your vision regularly. As you grow and change. your vision may evolve, and it's important to adjust it accordingly. Regularly reviewing your vision will also help you stay focused and motivated, as it reminds you of the bigger picture and the life you are working towards.

A STEP-BY-STEP GUIDE TO SETTING SMART GOALS

Setting SMART goals is a powerful way to turn your vision for the future into reality. SMART goals are specific, measurable, achievable, relevant, and time-bound, and they provide a clear roadmap for achieving your dreams. This step-by-step guide will walk you through the process of setting SMART goals and taking action to achieve them.

- Start with a Vision - Before you can set SMART goals, you need to have a clear vision for your future. This vision is your ultimate destination, and your goals are the steps that will take you there. Take some time to think about what you want your life to look like and what you want to achieve.
- Set Specific Goals - The first step in setting

SMART goals is to be specific about what you want to achieve. Instead of setting a vague goal like "I want to be successful." set a specific goal like "I want to earn a promotion to a management position within the next year." The more specific you are, the clearer your path will be.

- Make Your Goals Measurable - Once you have a specific goal in mind. The next step is to make it measurable. This means setting a clear outcome that you can track. Measurable goals allow you to track your progress and know when you've achieved them.
- Ensure Your Goals Are Achievable - It's important to set goals that are challenging but achievable. This means considering your current resources, capabilities, and limitations. Setting goals that are too ambitious can lead to frustration and disappointment if you don't achieve them. On the other hand, setting goals that are too easy may not push you to reach your full potential. Find a balance that challenges you while still being realistic.
- Make Your Goals Relevant - Your goals should be relevant to your overall vision and aligned with your values, passions, and long-term desires. When your goals are relevant, they are more likely to be meaningful and motivating.
- Set a Time Frame - The final step in setting SMART goals is to make them time-bound. This means setting a clear deadline for achieving your goals. A time frame creates a sense of urgency and helps you stay focused and motivated.
- Break Down Your Goals into Smaller Steps - The next step is to break them down into smaller and manageable steps. This makes your goals less overwhelming and helps you stay on track.
- Take Action - This means consistently working towards your goals, even when things get tough. It's important to stay focused and motivated, and to keep pushing forward, even in the face of challenges.
- Track Your Progress - Regularly tracking your progress is essential to achieving your SMART goals. This allows you to see how far you've come and to make any necessary adjustments along the way.
- Celebrate Your Successes - Finally, It's important to celebrate your successes along the way. Achieving your goals is a big accomplishment. This not only boosts your confidence but also motivates you to keep going and achieve even more.

STAYING MOTIVATED AND OVERCOMING CHALLENGES

Staying motivated is essential to achieving your goals and unlocking your full potential. However, Maintaining motivation can be challenging, especially when you face obstacles or setbacks. The key is to develop strategies that keep you focused and motivated, even when things get tough. One of the most effective ways to stay motivated is to keep your vision and goals at the forefront of your mind. This means regularly reviewing your vision and reminding yourself of why you set your goals in the first place. Keeping a vision board or writing down your goals and placing them somewhere you can see them every day can help you stay focused and motivated. Another important strategy for staying motivated is to break your goals down into smaller ones, manageable steps. When you break your goals down, they become less overwhelming and more achievable. Each small step you take brings you closer to your ultimate goal, and this sense of progress can help keep you motivated. It's also important to stay positive and focus on the things you can control.

There will always be challenges and setbacks along the way, but how you respond to them is what matters. Instead of dwelling on the things that go wrong, focus on the things you can do to move forward. This positive mindset will help you stay motivated and keep going, even when things get tough.

Another key to staying motivated is to surround yourself with positive influences. This means surrounding yourself with people who support and encourage you, and who believe in your ability to achieve your goals. Having a strong support system can make a big difference in your motivation and confidence. It's also important to take care of yourself, both physically and mentally. This means getting enough sleep, eating healthy, and taking time to relax and recharge. When you take care of yourself, you have more energy and motivation to pursue your goals. Finally, It's important to celebrate your successes along the way. Achieving your goals is a big accomplishment, and it's important to acknowledge and celebrate your hard work. This not only boosts your confidence but also motivates you to keep going and achieve even more.

BUILDING CONFIDENCE AND SELF-BELIEF

Confidence and self-belief are essential components of personal empowerment. When you believe in yourself and your abilities, you are more likely to take risks, pursue your goals, and overcome challenges. Building confidence and self-belief is a lifelong journey, but it is one that is well worth the effort. One of the first steps in building confidence is to focus on your strengths. Each of us has unique strengths and talents that make us who we are. By recognizing and embracing your strengths, you can build a strong foundation of self-belief. Make a list of your strengths and refer to it whenever you need a confidence boost. Another important aspect of building confidence is to challenge negative self-talk. Negative self-talk is the voice in your head that tells you that you're not good enough, smart enough, or capable enough. This voice is not based on reality, and it can hold you back from reaching your full potential. When you notice negative self-talk, challenge it by replacing it with positive affirmations. For example, instead of saying "I can't do this." say "I am capable and I can achieve anything I set my mind to." It's also important to step out of your comfort zone and take risks. Confidence is built through action, and the more you challenge yourself, the more your confidence will grow. Start by setting small goals that push you out of your comfort zone, and gradually work your way up to bigger challenges. Another key to building confidence is to focus on your achievements. Take time to reflect on the things you have accomplished in the past and the challenges you have overcome. This reflection will remind you of your capabilities and give you the confidence to take on new challenges. It's also important to practice self-compassion. This means being kind and understanding towards yourself, especially when things don't go as planned.

Remember that everyone makes mistakes and that setbacks are a normal part of the journey. Instead of being hard on yourself, practice self-compassion by treating yourself with the same kindness and understanding that you would offer a friend. Your body deserves love and care. Listen to it, nourish it with good food, and give it the rest it needs. Exercise should be about feeling strong and healthy, not punishing yourself. Find activities you enjoy and that make you feel good, whether it's dancing, swimming, or just taking a walk in nature. Your body is your lifelong companion, treat it with the respect it deserves.

CONFIDENCE-BUILDING TECHNIQUES THAT WORK

- Building confidence is a process, and there are several techniques that can help you along the way. These techniques are practical and effective, and they can help you build the confidence you need to pursue your goals and achieve your full potential.
- Practice Positive Affirmations - Repeat statements like "I am confident and capable" regularly to boost self-belief and reprogram your mind positively.
- Visualize Success - Imagine yourself achieving your goals. Visualization helps you stay focused and builds confidence by seeing yourself succeed.
- Set Small Goals - Start with small, achievable goals. Each success builds momentum and reinforces your belief in your abilities.
- Step Out of Your Comfort Zone - Take small risks to grow your confidence. Each step outside your comfort zone proves your capability to handle new challenges.
- Celebrate Your Successes - Recognize and celebrate each success. This boosts your

confidence and motivates you to keep striving for more.

- Practice Self-Care - Take care of your health by sleeping well, eating healthy, and exercising. Self-care gives you the energy to pursue your goals.
- Challenge Negative Self-Talk - Replace negative thoughts with affirmations like "I can do this." This helps overcome self-doubt and builds confidence.
- Surround Yourself with Positive Influences - Keep people around you who support and believe in you. Positive influences strengthen your self-belief.
- Focus on Your Strengths - Identify and concentrate on your unique strengths. This builds a solid foundation of confidence.

CONCLUSION: CELEBRATING YOUR INNER POWER

As you reach the end of this chapter, take a moment to reflect on the journey you've undertaken to embrace your inner power. You've explored what it truly means to be empowered, uncovered the depths of your inner strength, and learned how to unlock the vast potential that resides within you. You've discovered that empowerment is not just a fleeting feeling but a state of being—a way of life where you stand tall in your uniqueness, confident in your abilities, and ready to face challenges head-on. You've also gained practical tools to set and achieve your goals, ensuring that your vision for the future is not just a dream but a reality in the making. With each SMART goal you set and every obstacle you overcome, you're building a life that aligns with your true self—a life where your inner power guides you toward success and fulfillment. Finally, you've learned that confidence and self-belief are the cornerstones of empowerment. These qualities, like muscles, grow stronger the more you exercise them. By applying the confidence-building techniques shared in this chapter, you're continuously strengthening your belief in yourself and your capabilities. Now, as you continue your journey, remember to celebrate your inner power. It is a gift that will guide you through life's ups and downs, a source of strength that will never waver as long as you nurture it. Embrace this power, let it shine in all that you do. and know that you have everything within you to create a life that is not just lived. but truly celebrated.

Chapter 4

Building Meaningful Connections

Communication is the heartbeat of all relationships. Whether you're chatting with a best friend, talking to a parent. or meeting someone new. The way you express yourself can shape how that relationship grows. It's not just about what you say—it's also about how you listen, how you understand. and how you connect on a deeper level. You have strengths and abilities that are uniquely yours. Take a moment to think about what you're good at and what you enjoy doing. These strengths are the foundation of your inner power. When you focus on what you do well, you build confidence. and confidence is key to unlocking your potential.

COMMUNICATING WITH CONFIDENCE AND CLARITY

Have you ever held back from saying what's really on your mind because you weren't sure how it would be received? Or maybe you worried that your thoughts didn't matter? These are feelings we all experience at times, but learning to communicate with confidence can help you overcome them. When you speak with confidence, you're showing that you believe in what you're saying. It's not about being loud or forceful. It's about being sure of yourself. When you know that your thoughts and feelings are important. you're more likely to express them clearly, and clarity is key—when you say what you mean in a straightforward way. It helps others understand you better. Imagine you're in a group project at school. You have a great idea, but you're hesitant to share it because you're afraid it might not be well-received. Speaking up confidently, saying "I have an idea that could really help us out." and then clearly explaining your thoughts can make a big difference. Your team is more likely to take your ideas seriously when they see that you believe in them.

THE ART OF LISTENING AND UNDERSTANDING OTHERS

But communication isn't just about words. Have you ever noticed how someone's facial expression or the way they stand can tell you what they're feeling? even if they don't say a word? That's body language, and it's a powerful part of communication. When you're talking to someone. Your body language sends signals about how you're feeling and how engaged you are in the conversation. If you're slouching or avoiding eye contact, it might seem like you're not interested, even if you are. On the other hand, standing tall, smiling, and making eye contact shows that you're engaged and confident. For instance, when you're listening to a friend who's going through a tough time. leaning in slightly and nodding your head shows that you care about what they're saying. These little actions can make a big difference in how connected someone feels to you.

One of the most important parts of communication is listening—really listening. It's easy to get caught up in thinking about what you're going to say next or letting your mind wander, but when you truly focus on the person who's speaking. it shows that you value their words. Listening isn't just about hearing the words. It's about understanding the feelings behind them. Imagine a friend tells you they're feeling overwhelmed with school. Instead of just saying, "Yeah. That's tough." take a moment to really think about what they're going through. You might respond with something like. "That sounds really stressful. What's been the hardest part for you?" This shows that you're not just hearing them—you're trying to understand their experience. Listening like this can deepen your connections and make your relationships stronger. People appreciate it when they feel truly heard, and they're likely to trust you more and open up to you when they know you're someone who listens with care.

Building meaningful connections isn't just about communication—it's also about how we treat each other. Healthy relationships are built on respect, trust, and mutual understanding.

RECOGNIZING AND RESPECTING BOUNDARIES

Every relationship needs boundaries. These are the limits we set to protect our own well-being and respect others. Boundaries can be about anything—how much time you spend with someone, what topics you're comfortable discussing. or even physical space. For example, if you're someone who needs alone time to recharge, it's okay to let your friends know that sometimes you need a break. Saying, "I love hanging out with you, but I need some time to myself today." is a way of setting a boundary that helps you take care of your mental health. Respecting others' boundaries is just as important. If a friend tells you they're not ready to talk about something. It's important to respect that and give them the space they need. Healthy relationships thrive when both people feel safe and respected. Confidence doesn't mean you're perfect. It means you believe in yourself even when things are tough. Start by setting small goals that are achievable. Each time you reach a goal, no matter how small, you're proving to yourself that you can do it. Celebrate these victories, and let them remind you of your inner power.

BUILDING TRUST AND MUTUAL RESPECT

Trust is like the glue that holds relationships together. It's built over time, through actions that show you're reliable, honest, and caring. When you keep promises, show up when you say you will, and are honest even when it's hard, you're building trust with the people around you. Let's say you've promised a friend you'll help them study for a big test. Following through on that promise, even if you're busy, shows that they can rely on you. Over time, these small actions build a strong foundation of trust that can make your relationship unshakeable. Trust also means being able to share your thoughts and feelings without fear of judgment. When a friend confides in you, it's important to listen without criticizing or belittling their experience. This creates a safe space where both of you can be yourselves.

Navigating Social Situations with Ease

Social situations can sometimes be challenging, especially if you struggle with anxiety or shyness. But with some practice and the right mindset, you can navigate these situations with more ease and confidence. We all have moments of doubt, but it's important not to let them hold you back. When you hear that little voice in your head telling you you're not good enough, challenge it. Remind yourself of the times you've succeeded and the strengths you possess. You are capable of amazing things, and your potential is limitless, Words have power. Positive affirmations are a way to remind yourself of your worth and capabilities. Try saying something like,"I am strong. I am capable. I am worthy of love and respect." Say it out loud, write it down, or even create a mantra that you repeat to yourself each day. Over time, these affirmations can reshape how you see yourself and the world around you.

TIPS FOR OVERCOMING SOCIAL ANXIETY

It's natural to feel nervous in social situations. especially if you're meeting new people or speaking in front of a group. Social anxiety is something many people experience, and it's okay to feel this way. The key is to find strategies that help you manage those feelings so they don't hold you back. One way to cope with social anxiety is to focus on the present moment. When you start to feel anxious, take a deep breath and remind yourself that you're okay. Instead of worrying about what others might think, try to focus on the conversation or the activity you're involved in. For example, if you're at a party and start feeling overwhelmed, find a quiet spot where you can take a few deep breaths. Then, try to re-engage in a way that feels comfortable for you. Maybe you start a conversation with someone who's standing alone, or you join a smaller group where you feel more at ease. It can also help to challenge negative thoughts. If you're thinking, "Everyone is going to judge me." try to replace that thought with something more realistic. like, "Most people are too focused on themselves to notice everything I do." By reframing your thoughts, you can reduce some of the anxiety that comes with social situations.

DEVELOPING A STRONG SUPPORT NETWORK

Having a strong support network is essential for navigating life's challenges. This network can include family, friends, teachers, or anyone you trust and feel comfortable turning to when you need help or advice. Building a support network isn't just about having people to rely on when times are tough. It's also about surrounding yourself with positive influences who encourage you to grow and be your best self. These are the people who cheer you on, who give you honest feedback. and who is there for you, no matter what. To build a strong support network, focus on nurturing the relationships that matter most to you. Spend time with people who lift you up, and don't be afraid to reach out when you need support. Remember, It's okay to lean on others, just as it's okay for them to lean on you.

THE IMPACT OF SELF-LOVE ON RELATIONSHIPS

The way you relate to yourself significantly impacts how you relate to others. When you practice self-love, you set a positive example for your relationships. You're more likely to approach interactions with confidence, empathy, and respect, which fosters healthier and more fulfilling connections. Self-love helps you set healthy boundaries and communicate effectively. It allows you to express your needs and desires clearly while respecting the needs of others. By loving yourself. You also teach others how to treat you, setting the standard for how you expect to be treated in relationships. Here are some ways self-love influences your relationships:

- Self-Respect: When you value yourself, you're less likely to tolerate disrespect or mistreatment from others. You know that you deserve to be treated with kindness and consideration.
- Healthy Boundaries: Self-love empowers you to set and maintain boundaries that protect your well-being. You understand the importance of saying no when necessary and ensuring that your relationships are mutually respectful.
- Effective Communication: Loving yourself helps you communicate more effectively. You're able to express your thoughts and feelings clearly and listen empathetically to others.
- Conflict Resolution: Self-love enables you to approach conflicts with a balanced perspective. You're more likely to seek constructive solutions and work towards mutual understanding.
- Mutual Support: In healthy relationships. Both parties support and uplift each other. When you love yourself, you're better equipped to offer support and encouragement to others.

Take time to reflect on your current relationships and how they align with your sense of self-love. Consider how your self-worth influences your interactions and whether there are areas where you can improve your relationships through self-love and healthy communication. Self-love plays a crucial role in setting and achieving goals. When you believe in yourself and your abilities you're more likely to set ambitious goals and take the necessary steps to achieve them. Self-love provides the confidence and motivation needed to pursue your dreams with determination and resilience. Start by creating a clear vision of what you want to achieve. Visualize your goals and imagine the steps needed to reach them. Self-love helps you stay focused on your vision and motivates you to take action, even when faced with obstacles. Strategies for achieving your goals:

- Set specific, measurable, and achievable goals that align with your values and aspirations. Clearly define what success looks like for each goal.
- Create a detailed plan outlining the steps required to achieve your goals. Break down large goals into smaller ones, manageable tasks to maintain motivation and track progress.
- Maintain commitment to your goals by regularly reviewing your progress and adjusting your plan as needed. Self-love helps you stay focused and persevere through challenges.
- Acknowledge and celebrate your achievements, no matter how small. Recognizing your successes reinforces your sense of self-worth and encourages continued effort.
- Use setbacks as learning opportunities rather than as reasons to give up. Reflect on what went wrong, adjust your approach, and continue moving forward with renewed determination.

Consider building a support system to help you achieve your goals. Share your aspirations with trusted friends, family members, or mentors who can offer guidance, encouragement, and accountability.

CONCLUSION: THE JOY OF GENUINE CONNECTIONS

There's something incredibly special about having meaningful connections in your life. Whether it's the comfort of a deep friendship, the support of a caring family member, or the fun of hanging out with people who "get" you. These connections bring joy and fulfillment. Friendships and community are sources of strength and happiness. They provide a sense of belonging and remind you that you're not alone in the world. Embrace these connections with an open heart, and don't be afraid to show your friends and community how much they mean to you. Cherish the moments of laughter, the shared experiences, and even the tough times you go through together. These are the things that create bonds that last a lifetime. As you move forward, continue to build and nurture the relationships that matter to you. Don't be afraid to put yourself out there, to show kindness, and to open your heart to new connections. Every relationship is an opportunity to learn, grow, and experience the beauty of human connection. Navigating social situations can sometimes feel overwhelming. especially when you're faced with new experiences or unfamiliar groups. It's normal to feel unsure or even anxious, but standing strong in these situations is about staying true to who you are and believing in your own worth.

One of the biggest challenges in social settings is the pressure to fit in. You might feel like you need to change something about yourself to be accepted or liked. But the truth is, the most meaningful connections happen when you're being authentic. When you're true to yourself, you attract people who appreciate you for who you really are. Think about a time when you met someone new and immediately felt comfortable around them. Chances are, they were being their true selves, Which made you feel at ease to be yourself too. That's the kind of connection you want to aim for—a relationship built on honesty and mutual respect. Being yourself doesn't mean you won't ever feel nervous or out of place. It's okay to have those feelings, but remember that you don't need to pretend to be someone else to fit in. The right people will appreciate the real you.

Finding Your Place in a Community - Being part of a community gives you a sense of connection to something bigger than yourself. It's a place where you can contribute, learn, and grow alongside others. Finding your place in a community starts with getting involved and showing up. Think about the communities you're already part of—maybe it's a club at school, a sports team, or a volunteer group. What do you enjoy about being part of these groups? How do they make you feel? When you actively participate in your community, you're building relationships and creating a support network that can help you through all kinds of experiences.

Contributing to Your Community - One of the most rewarding aspects of being part of a community is the opportunity to contribute. Whether it's helping out with a project, offering your skills, or simply being a supportive presence. Your contributions can make a big difference. For example, if you're part of a club or team, offering to help organize events or lead activities can be a great way to get more involved. Not only does this strengthen your ties to the group, but it also gives you a chance to develop new skills and build confidence. Being an active member of your community also means being there for others. Just like in friendships, showing kindness, offering support, and being a positive influence can create a ripple effect that strengthens the entire group.

Building Meaningful Connections in Your Community - As you contribute to your community, you'll find that you naturally build connections with others. These connections can be just as meaningful as your close friendships, offering support, collaboration, and a sense of belonging. Whether it's working together on a school project, volunteering at a local event, or simply being a friendly face in the crowd. The connections you build in your community can enrich your life in many ways. These relationships broaden your perspective, introduce you to new experiences, and help you feel more connected to the world around you.

Building meaningful connections is a journey that enriches every aspect of your life. From deep friendships to being part of a supportive community. These relationships provide joy, support, and a sense of belonging that helps you thrive. As you continue on your journey, remember that the key to strong relationships is authenticity, trust, and respect—both for yourself and for others. Embrace who you are, stand strong in your values, and open your heart to the connections that bring out the best in you. Cherish the friends who make you laugh, the communities that welcome you, and the moments of genuine connection that remind you of the beauty of human relationships. These are the ties that make life rich and meaningful, and they are worth nurturing every step of the way.

Chapter 5

Standing Strong Against Peer Pressure

Peer pressure is one of the most challenging aspects of growing up, particularly during the teenage years. As you begin to carve out your own identity and navigate the complexities of social dynamics. The influence of peers can be both a positive and negative force. Understanding peer pressure, how it manifests, and developing the skills to resist it are crucial steps in asserting your individuality and making choices that align with your true self.

Understanding Peer Pressure

Peer pressure can be subtle or overt, but its impact can be profound. It's the influence that people your age exert on you, whether intentionally or unintentionally. This pressure can push you to conform to group norms, engage in behaviors you might not otherwise choose, or adopt attitudes that don't align with your personal values. There are many forms of peer pressure. Some are direct, like when a friend urges you to try something you're uncomfortable with. Others are indirect, such as feeling the need to dress a certain way because everyone else is doing it. It can also be positive when friends encourage you to study harder or pursue a healthy hobby. However, The negative forms of peer pressure can be particularly challenging to resist because they often play on our desires to fit in, be liked, and avoid conflict. One of the first steps in standing strong against peer pressure is understanding its roots. Peer pressure often stems from the human need for belonging. During adolescence, this need is particularly acute. You're not just figuring out who you are, you're also trying to find your place in the social world. The opinions of peers can start to feel like the most important thing, sometimes even more significant than your own beliefs or the values you've been raised with. But here's the truth: your self-worth isn't determined by how well you fit in with others, but by how true you remain to yourself. Every time you resist negative peer pressure, you're reinforcing your own identity and setting the foundation for the person you'll become. One of the most empowering things you can do in the face of peer pressure is to find and use your voice. This means being able to speak up for yourself, to say no when something doesn't feel right, and to express your opinions and feelings without fear of judgment. Finding your voice isn't always easy. It takes practice and courage, especially if you're used to going along with the crowd. But the more you practice asserting yourself. the easier it becomes. It starts with small steps—like voicing your opinion in a group discussion or politely declining an invitation to something you're not comfortable with. Over time, as you get more comfortable with standing up for yourself, you'll find that it becomes second nature, and the more you use your voice, the more confident you'll feel In your ability to make decisions that are right for you, not just what's expected of you.

One way to start finding your voice is by identifying your core values. What's important to you? What do you believe in? When you have a clear understanding of your values, it becomes easier to make decisions that align with them. For example, if you value honesty, you'll feel more confident in speaking up when something doesn't feel right. Or if you value kindness, you might feel more comfortable standing up for someone who's being treated unfairly. Another way to strengthen your voice is by practicing self-advocacy. This means standing up for your needs and rights, whether it's in your relationships, at school, or in other areas of your life. Self-advocacy is about knowing what you need and being willing to ask for it, even when it's uncomfortable. It's about recognizing that your voice matters and that you deserve to be heard. Good communication is the foundation of any relationship, whether it's with friends, family, or new people you meet. It's about more than just talking. It's also about listening and understanding. When you communicate openly and honestly, you build trust and strengthen your connections with others. True friends are those who support you, uplift you, and accept you for who you are. It's important to surround yourself with people who bring out the best in you. Building healthy friendships involves being a good friend in return—listening, being supportive, and respecting each other's boundaries.

DIFFERENT KINDS OF PEER PRESSURE

Peer pressure comes in many shapes and forms. and recognizing these different types can help you better prepare to deal with them.

- Direct Peer Pressure: This is the most obvious form, where someone explicitly tells you what to do. It might come in the form of a dare, a challenge, or simply a request. For example, a friend might directly ask you to skip school, drink alcohol, or participate in bullying. The key to resisting direct peer pressure is having the confidence to say no firmly and clearly, Remember, your true friends will respect your boundaries and decisions.
- Indirect Peer Pressure - Indirect peer pressure is more subtle but can be just as powerful. It occurs when you feel the need to conform to the behaviors and expectations of a group without anyone explicitly asking you to do so. For instance, if everyone in your friend group starts dressing a certain way. you might feel pressured to do the same. even if that style doesn't feel like "you." Understanding that your worth is not tied to how well you conform to others' expectations is crucial in resisting indirect peer pressure.
- Positive Peer Pressure - Not all peer pressure is negative. Positive peer pressure is when your friends encourage you to make good decisions. such as studying for a test, participating in a new activity, or standing up for someone being bullied. Surrounding yourself with friends who exert positive peer pressure can help you grow and develop in positive ways.
- Negative Peer Pressure - This is when the influence of others leads you to make poor choices or engage in harmful behaviors. Negative peer pressure might encourage you to engage in risky activities, skip school, or participate in gossip and bullying. Learning to identify and resist negative peer pressure is critical for maintaining your integrity and self-respect.
- Dealing with FOMO (Fear of Missing Out) - One of the biggest drivers of peer pressure is FOMO—the fear of missing out. It's that nagging feeling that if you don't go along with what everyone else is doing, you'll be left out, or worse, forgotten. FOMO can make it incredibly hard to say no, even when you know that what's being offered

isn't right for you. But here's the truth: missing out on something that doesn't align with who you are is actually a win, not a loss. When you say no to things that don't serve you, you're making room for things that do. It's about prioritizing your own happiness and well-being over the temporary satisfaction of fitting in. When you feel FOMO creeping in, remind yourself that you're making the choice that's best for you, and that's something to be proud of. The people who truly matter in your life will respect your decisions, and those who don't aren't worth your time or energy. To help combat FOMO, try shifting your focus from what you're missing out on to what you're gaining. For example, if you decide to stay home instead of going to a party that doesn't interest you, think about the benefits—maybe you'll get some much-needed rest, spend quality time with your family, or work on a hobby you love. By focusing on the positives, you can reframe your mindset and reduce the power of FOMO over your decisions.

- Understanding these different forms of peer pressure can help you identify when you're being influenced and give you the tools to respond in a way that aligns with your values. Every experience with peer pressure, whether positive or negative. is an opportunity to learn more about yourself. It's a chance to reflect on what's important to you, to test your boundaries, and to strengthen your resolve. When you face peer pressure, take a moment to think about what you've learned. Did you discover something new about your values? Did you find out that you're stronger than you thought? Use these experiences to build a deeper understanding of yourself and to prepare for future challenges. Remember, every time you resist negative peer pressure, you're reinforcing your own identity and strengthening your ability to make choices that are right for you, and every time you embrace positive peer pressure, you're opening yourself up to new opportunities for growth and self-improvement. It's also important to remember that peer pressure is a normal part of life. Everyone experiences it at some point, and it's something you'll continue to encounter even as you grow older. But the more you learn about yourself and the stronger you become in your convictions, the easier it will be to navigate these pressures and stay true to who you are.

HOW TO IDENTIFY AND RESPOND TO PEER PRESSURE

Identifying peer pressure isn't always easy, especially when it comes in subtle forms. However, There are signs you can watch for, if you feel uncomfortable. I'm anxious, or conflicted about a situation. It's a good indicator that you're facing peer pressure. Your gut feeling is often your best guide. If something doesn't feel right, it probably isn't. Responding to peer pressure involves several key strategies:

- Your instincts are your internal guide. When you feel that something isn't right. It's important to listen to that feeling.
- It's essential to know what your boundaries are before you find yourself in a situation where they might be tested. Take some time to think about your values and what's important to you. When you have a clear understanding of your boundaries, it's easier to communicate them to others.
- Saying no can be difficult, especially when you don't want to disappoint your friends or seem like the odd one out. However, Being firm in your refusal is critical. You don't have to be rude or confrontational, simple, confident "No, thanks. I'm not into that." can be enough. It's important to stand your ground and not let others sway your decision.
- If you find yourself in a situation where the pressure is too intense. It's okay to walk away. Removing yourself from a situation that feels wrong is a sign of strength, not weakness. Whether it's leaving a party where drugs are being used or stepping away from a group of friends who are bullying someone. Your well-being is more important than fitting in.

These strategies might seem straightforward, but in the heat of the moment, they can be hard to remember. Practice them in your mind beforehand, so when the time comes, you're prepared.

HOW TO STAY TRUE TO YOURSELF

The first step in staying true to yourself is knowing who you are. This means understanding your values, beliefs and what's important to you. Take some time to reflect on what matters most in your life. What are your goals? What do you believe in? What kind of person do you want to be? The more you know about yourself, the easier it will be to stay true to your values when faced with peer pressure. Self-confidence is key to resisting peer pressure. When you believe in yourself and your decisions, it becomes easier to stand up for what you believe in. Confidence doesn't come overnight, but you can build it through positive self-talk, setting and achieving goals, and surrounding yourself with supportive people. Remember, it's okay to make mistakes. What's important is learning from them and continuing to grow. Sometimes, staying true to yourself means standing up for what you believe in. even when others don't agree. This can be challenging, especially if you're going against the crowd.

However, standing up for your beliefs is a sign of integrity and strength. It's about being honest with yourself and others. You might say "I don't feel comfortable doing that." or "That doesn't align with my values." It's not always easy, but it's important to stay true to yourself. When you stand up for yourself, you might face pushback from others. They might try to convince you to change your mind or make you feel like you're overreacting. It's important to be prepared for this and to stand firm in your decision. Remember, you don't owe anyone an explanation for your choices. You have the right to make decisions that are best for you, regardless of what others think. Your inner strength is your most powerful tool in resisting peer pressure. This strength comes from knowing who you are, what you stand for, and having the confidence to live by your values. It's about being true to yourself, even when it's difficult. Every time you resist peer pressure, you're building your inner strength and reinforcing your sense of self.

Staying true to yourself isn't always easy, but it's one of the most important things you can do for your mental and emotional well-being. By knowing yourself, building your confidence, standing up for your beliefs, being prepared for pushback, and finding your inner strength, you can navigate peer pressure with grace and integrity. It's natural to want to fit in, but remember that it's okay to say no to things that don't align with your values or make you uncomfortable. Peer pressure can be tough, but staying true to yourself is always more important than pleasing others. Practice assertiveness by calmly and confidently expressing your feelings. The right friends will respect your decisions. Empathy is about understanding and sharing the feelings of others. It's a powerful skill that helps you connect with people on a deeper level. Try to put yourself in others' shoes and consider how they might be feeling. When you approach relationships with empathy, you build stronger, more meaningful connections.

Resisting negative influences isn't just about saying no. It's about actively choosing what's best for you, even when it's not the easiest option. Here are some strategies to help you resist negative influences and stay true to your values.

- Your values guide your decisions and help you stay true to yourself; clarity on them aids in making aligned choices.
- Surround yourself with friends who share your values, as positive friendships support your growth, while negative ones can mislead you.
- Assertiveness involves confidently and respectfully setting boundaries, helping you resist negative influences without being confrontational.
- Consider your long-term goals when facing peer pressure; align decisions with your future aspirations to support success.
- Reflect on past mistakes as learning opportunities, using them to develop strategies for resisting future pressure.
- A strong support system of like-minded friends, family, or mentors can provide guidance and encouragement in resisting negative influences.

These strategies can help you stay true to yourself and resist negative influences. Remember, you have the power to make decisions that are best for you, even when it's difficult.

ASSERTIVENESS: YOUR SUPERPOWER

Assertiveness is one of the most powerful tools you have in resisting peer pressure. It's about expressing your thoughts. feelings, and beliefs are clear, direct, and in a respectful way. Assertiveness allows you to stand up for yourself without being aggressive or passive. Being assertive means knowing your rights and not being afraid to speak up for them. It's about setting boundaries and being clear about what you will and won't do. For example, if someone is pressuring you to do something you're uncomfortable with. Being assertive might mean saying, "I don't want to do that. and I won't be pressured into it." It's not always easy, but with practice, you can develop the confidence to stand up for yourself in any situation. One of the keys to assertiveness is believing in your own worth. You have the right to make decisions that are best for you, regardless of what others might think. When you're confident in your own worth, it's easier to be assertive and resist peer pressure. Another important aspect of assertiveness is knowing when to walk away. If someone continues to pressure you after you've clearly stated your boundaries, it's okay to remove yourself from the situation. Walking away isn't a sign of weakness. It's a sign of strength and self-respect. You have the right to protect your well-being and to distance yourself from people who don't respect your boundaries. Assertiveness is a skill that you can develop over time. Start by practicing in low-pressure situations, like telling a friend that you'd rather not go to a certain movie or restaurant. As you become more comfortable with assertiveness, you'll find it easier to use in more challenging situations.

TAKING A STAND FOR YOURSELF AND OTHERS

Taking a stand for yourself is crucial, but so is standing up for others. Peer pressure often affects more than just you. It can influence your friends and classmates as well. Standing up for what's right, even when it's difficult, is a sign of true leadership. When you take a stand for others, you're showing that you're not just thinking about yourself. but about the well-being of those around you. For example, if you see someone being bullied or pressured into doing something they're uncomfortable with, you can step in and offer your support. This might mean speaking up and saying, "Hey. that's not okay." or simply being there for the person who's being pressured. Taking a stand for others doesn't mean you have to be confrontational or put yourself in a dangerous situation. It's about offering support, showing empathy, and standing up for what's right. Your actions can have a powerful impact on others and can help create a more positive and supportive environment for everyone.

Making Choices That Align with Your Values

Making choices that align with your values is one of the most important things you can do to stay true to yourself. Your values are the principles and beliefs that guide your decisions and actions. When you make choices that align with your values, you're living in a way that's true to who you are. To make choices that align with your values. It's important to take some time to reflect on what those values are. Think about what's most important to you in life. Is it honesty? Compassion? Responsibility? Once you're clear on your values, use them as a guide when making decisions. For example, if you value honesty, you might choose not to participate in gossip or lying, even if others around you are doing so, If you value kindness, you might choose to stand up for someone who's being treated unfairly. By making choices that align with your values, you're staying true to yourself and living with integrity. It's not always easy to make choices that align with your values, especially when you're facing peer pressure. However, by staying true to your values, you're building a strong sense of self and creating a life that reflects who you are.

UNDERSTANDING THE IMPACT OF YOUR DECISIONS

Every decision you make has an impact. not just on you, but on those around you as well. It's important to consider the potential consequences of your actions before making a decision. For example, if you're being pressured to try drugs or alcohol. It's important to think about the potential impact on your health, your relationships, and your future. How might this decision affect your goals? your well-being, and your ability to be the person you want to be? Understanding the impact of your decisions also means thinking about how your actions might affect others. For example, if you choose to stand up against bullying, you're not just protecting yourself, but you're also helping to create a safer and more positive environment for everyone. By taking the time to consider the potential impact of your decisions, you can make choices that are in line with your values and that support your overall well-being.

BUILDING RESILIENCE AGAINST ADVERSE IMPACTS

Resilience is the ability to bounce back from challenges and setbacks. It's about developing the inner strength to overcome adversity and continue moving forward, even when things get tough. Building resilience against adverse impacts means developing the skills and mindset to resist peer pressure and recover from difficult situations. Here are some ways to build resilience:

- Practice Self-Care - Taking care of yourself is crucial for building resilience. This means getting enough sleep, eating well, staying active, and taking time to relax and recharge. When you're physically and emotionally healthy, you're better equipped to handle challenges and resist peer pressure.
- Develop a Growth Mindset - A growth mindset is the belief that you can learn and grow from your experiences, even when things don't go as planned. Instead of seeing setbacks as failures, view them as opportunities to learn and improve. This mindset can help you build resilience and stay positive, even in the face of adversity.
- Surround Yourself with Supportive People - Having a strong support system is key to building resilience. Surround yourself with friends, family, and mentors who believe in you and support your goals. These people can offer guidance, encouragement, and a listening ear when you're facing challenges.
- Practice Problem-Solving Skills - Resilience involves being able to think critically and solve problems effectively. When you're faced with a challenge, take the time to consider your options and come up with a plan. Practicing problem-solving skills can help you build confidence and resilience.
- Stay Positive - Maintaining a positive outlook can help you build resilience and overcome challenges. Focus on your strengths, celebrate your successes, and remind yourself of your goals and values. Staying positive doesn't mean ignoring difficulties. It means approaching them with a hopeful and proactive mindset.

Building resilience takes time. but it's an important skill that will serve you well throughout your life. By practicing self-care. developing a growth mindset, surrounding yourself with supportive people, practicing problem-solving skills, and staying positive, you can build the resilience you need to resist peer pressure and overcome challenges.

EMBRACING YOUR RIGHT TO CHOOSE WHAT'S BEST FOR YOU

You have the right to make decisions that are best for you, regardless of what others might think. This right is fundamental to your well-being and personal growth. It's about recognizing that you are the author of your own life and that you have the power to choose your path. Embracing your right to choose means trusting yourself and your instincts. It's about believing in your ability to make decisions that are in line with your values and goals. It also means respecting your own boundaries and not letting others pressure you into doing something that doesn't feel right. One of the most powerful ways to embrace your right to choose is to practice self-advocacy. Self-advocacy is the ability to speak up for yourself and assert your needs and rights. This might mean saying no to peer pressure, asking for help when you need it, or making decisions that are best for you, even when others don't agree. Embracing your right to choose also means accepting responsibility for your decisions. When you make a choice, you're taking ownership of your life and your future. This responsibility is empowering because it means that you have the power to shape your life in a way that reflects who you are and what you believe in.

Personal Stories: Overcoming Peer Pressure

To make this chapter more relatable and engaging. Let's explore some personal stories of teen girls who have faced and overcome peer pressure. These stories highlight the challenges of resisting peer pressure and the strength it takes to stay true to oneself.

EMILY'S STAND AGAINST BULLYING

Emily was always the quiet one in her group of friends. She didn't like to draw attention to herself and preferred to go along with whatever everyone else was doing. But one day, she witnessed something that made her question her silence. One of the girls in Emily's class. Sarah was being bullied by a group of popular girls. They teased her about her clothes, her hair, and even the way she talked. Emily watched as Sarah tried to laugh it off. but she could see the pain in her eyes. Emily wanted to say something, but the fear of being targeted herself kept her quiet. But as the days went on, the bullying continued and Emily couldn't stand it any longer. She knew that staying silent made her complicit, and she didn't want to be part of a group that made others feel bad about themselves. So. one day when the bullying started again. Emily spoke up. She told the girls to stop and that what they were doing was wrong. The popular girls laughed and told her to mind her own business, but Emily didn't back down. She stood by Sarah and told the bullies that if they didn't stop, she would report them to the teacher. Emily's actions had a ripple effect. Other students started to speak up, and the bullying eventually stopped. Sarah was grateful for Emily's support, and the two became close friends. Emily learned that standing up for others was just as important as standing up for herself and that sometimes. It only takes one person to make a difference.

JESSICA'S STRUGGLE WITH BODY IMAGE

Jessica had always been self-conscious about her body. She was taller than most of the girls in her class, and she often felt awkward and out of place. Her friends were constantly talking about diets and workouts, and Jessica felt the pressure to change her body to fit in. She started skipping meals and spending hours at the gym, all in an effort to lose weight. But no matter how much weight she lost, she never felt good enough. The pressure to look a certain way was overwhelming, and Jessica began to feel like she would never be able to meet her friends' expectations. One day, Jessica's best friend Mia. noticed how much Jessica was struggling, Mia had always been supportive of Jessica, but she hadn't realized the extent of the pressure Jessica was feeling. Mia told Jessica that she didn't need to change her body to fit in, and that she was beautiful just the way she was. This conversation was a turning point for Jessica. She realized that she had been putting too much pressure on herself to meet unrealistic standards and that her worth wasn't determined by her appearance, with Mia's support. Jessica started to focus on her health and well-being, rather than trying to change her body to fit in. Jessica's journey to self-acceptance wasn't easy, but it taught her an important lesson about the dangers of peer pressure and the importance of loving herself for who she was.

CONCLUSION: EMPOWERING YOURSELF AND OTHERS

Peer pressure is an integral part of growing up, especially during the teenage years. It's a time when you're actively figuring out who you are, and the influence of your peers can feel incredibly strong. Whether it's about how you look, the things you like, or the choices you make. Peer pressure is everywhere. But it's crucial to understand that peer pressure is not just about giving in to the demands of others—it's also about understanding its power over your decisions and finding ways to navigate through it while staying true to yourself. As a teen girl, Peer pressure can manifest in countless ways. You might feel the need to dress a certain way because your friends do, or maybe you feel pressured to join in on activities you're not comfortable with just to fit in. Sometimes, It's about the music you listen to, the people you hang out with, or even the way you talk. The pressure to conform can be overwhelming, and it's easy to feel like everyone else has it all figured out. But here's the thing—everyone feels peer pressure. It's a shared experience, even for those who seem the most confident. The trick is not to let it control your decisions but to understand it, recognize its forms, and learn how to deal with it in a way that allows you to stay connected to your true self. Standing strong against peer pressure is one of the most important skills you can develop as a teenager. It's about knowing yourself, staying true to your values, and having the confidence to make decisions that are best for you. By understanding the different forms of peer pressure, building resilience, practicing assertiveness, and embracing your right to choose, you can navigate the challenges of adolescence with integrity and strength. Remember, you are not alone in this journey. There are people who care about you and want to see you succeed. Don't be afraid to reach out for support when you need it. By staying true to yourself and making choices that align with your values, you're building a foundation for happiness, healthy, and fulfilling life.

Chapter 6

Managing Stress and Embracing Calm

Identifying Sources Of Stress and Anxiety

As you navigate through your teenage years, it's completely normal to encounter various forms of stress and anxiety. Life is full of challenges, and during this time, it feels like everything is changing—your body, your emotions, your relationships, and even your responsibilities. Stress can come from multiple directions, and sometimes, it might feel like it's too much to handle. But understanding where your stress is coming from is the first step in learning how to manage it effectively.

One of the most common sources of stress during these years is academic pressure. Whether it's preparing for exams, completing assignments, or trying to maintain good grades, the expectations can weigh heavily on you. It's not just about wanting to do well; it's about the fear of failure, the worry that your future might be at stake if you don't perform as expected. This kind of pressure can make you feel like you're constantly racing against the clock, with no room for mistakes. Social dynamics also play a significant role in teenage stress. Friendships during this time can be incredibly fulfilling, but they can also be a source of anxiety. You might worry about fitting in, about what others think of you, or about the changing nature of your relationships.

Social media can amplify these concerns, as it often seems like everyone else's life is perfect while you're struggling with your own challenges. The need to project a certain image online can add to the stress, making you feel like you're always on display. Family expectations are another common stressor. Parents and guardians usually want what's best for you,

but their expectations can sometimes feel overwhelming. They might push you to excel in school, participate in extracurricular activities, or start planning for your future career. While these expectations come from a place of love and care, they can feel like added pressure, especially if you're struggling to meet them or if your interests don't align with what's expected.

Another significant source of stress is body image and self-esteem. During your teenage years, your body goes through many changes, and it's natural to feel self-conscious. The media often portrays unrealistic standards of beauty, which can make you feel like you don't measure up. This can lead to a constant worry about your appearance, your weight, or how others perceive you, which can be exhausting and stressful. The uncertainty of the future is another common concern.

As you get closer to the end of high school, the pressure to figure out what comes next can be intense. Whether it's deciding on a college, a career path, or even just thinking about your place in the world, the future can seem both exciting and terrifying. The fear of making the wrong choice or not living up to expectations can create a lot of anxiety. Understanding these sources of stress is important because it allows you to recognize that what you're feeling is normal. Everyone faces these challenges in one way or another, and acknowledging them is the first step toward managing stress effectively.

TEENAGE COMMON TRIGGERS

Stress is your body's way of responding to any kind of demand or threat. When you feel threatened, your nervous system responds by releasing a flood of stress hormones, including adrenaline and cortisol, which prepare the body for emergency action. This is known as the "fight-or-flight" response. However, when this response is triggered too often by everyday life, it can lead to chronic stress, which isn't healthy for your body or mind. In your teenage years, several factors can trigger stress:

- Academic Pressure: Tests, exams, homework, and the pressure to perform well can be major sources of stress. You might feel like your entire future depends on your grades, and this can weigh heavily on your mind.
- Social Dynamics: Friendships, relationships, and the social scene in general can be tricky to navigate. Whether it's fitting in, dealing with peer pressure, or handling conflicts, social situations can often cause stress.
- Family Expectations: Sometimes, parents and family members have high expectations for you. They may want you to excel in school, participate in extracurricular activities, or follow a certain career path. While their intentions are usually good, the pressure can be overwhelming.
- Body Image and Self-Esteem: Growing up comes with a lot of changes, especially in how you see yourself. You might feel stressed about your appearance, weight, or the way others perceive you.
- Future Uncertainty: As you get older, you might start to worry about the future. Questions like, "What will I do after high school?" or "What career path should I choose?" can create a lot of anxiety.

Understanding these triggers is the first step in managing your stress. It's important to remember that you're not alone—many teens experience these same challenges, and it's okay to feel overwhelmed sometimes.

SIGNS YOU MIGHT BE OVERWHELMED

Stress can manifest in various ways, and it's crucial to recognize the signs before it spirals out of control. Being aware of these signs allows you to take action early, preventing stress from negatively affecting your health and well-being. Stress manifests in many ways, and sometimes it can sneak up on you without you even realizing it. It's essential to be aware of the signs that indicate you might be overwhelmed so you can address the stress before it becomes too much to handle. Emotionally, stress can cause irritability or frequent mood swings. You might find yourself getting upset over small things or feeling unusually sensitive. One moment, everything seems fine, and the next, you're on edge, snapping at someone or feeling like

you're about to cry. These sudden emotional shifts can be confusing and frustrating, both for you and for those around you.

Another emotional sign of stress is a constant feeling of being overwhelmed. You might feel like you have too much to do and not enough time or energy to do it all. This sense of being buried under responsibilities can lead to feelings of helplessness or despair. You might even start to dread activities or tasks that you used to enjoy because they now feel like burdens. Anxiety or constant worrying is another common sign of stress. You might find yourself thinking about all the things that could go wrong, even when there's no immediate threat. This constant state of worry can be exhausting, making it hard to focus on the present because your mind is always racing toward potential problems in the future. Stress can also lead to feelings of depression or apathy. You might lose interest in activities that once brought you joy or feel like nothing really matters anymore. This sense of hopelessness can make it difficult to motivate yourself to do anything, leading to a cycle of inactivity and further stress. Physically, stress can manifest in various ways. Fatigue is a common symptom, where you feel tired all the time, even if you're getting enough sleep. This exhaustion can make it hard to concentrate or stay motivated. Headaches and migraines are also frequent physical responses to stress, often caused by tension in your neck and shoulders. Stomach issues are another physical sign of stress. You might experience stomach aches, nausea, or other digestive problems, especially when you're feeling particularly anxious. Stress can also disrupt your sleep, causing you to have trouble falling asleep, staying asleep, or feeling rested even after a full night's sleep.

Changes in appetite can also be a sign of stress. Some people lose their appetite when they're stressed, while others might overeat, particularly foods that are high in sugar or fat. Both of these responses can negatively impact your health and well-being. Behaviorally, stress can lead to procrastination, where you put off tasks because they feel too overwhelming. While procrastination might provide temporary relief, it usually adds to your stress in the long run when deadlines start to pile up. Stress can also cause you to withdraw from social activities, isolating yourself from friends and family because you feel too exhausted or anxious to interact with others. Unhealthy coping mechanisms, such as excessive screen time, overeating, or substance use, can also be signs that stress is taking a toll on you. These behaviors might offer temporary comfort, but they can lead to bigger problems down the line. Recognizing these signs is crucial because they serve as your body's way of telling you that something isn't right. If you notice these symptoms, it's important to take action to address the underlying stress before it becomes more serious.

Emotional Signs:

- Irritability or Moodiness: Do you find yourself getting easily annoyed or snapping at others over small things? This could be a sign of stress.
- Feeling Overwhelmed: If you often feel like everything is too much to handle, you might be dealing with stress.
- Anxiety or Worrying: Constantly worrying about things, even when there's no immediate threat, is a clear indicator of stress.

Physical Signs:

- Fatigue: Stress can leave you feeling exhausted, even if you haven't done anything particularly strenuous.
- Headaches: Frequent headaches or migraines can be a physical manifestation of stress.
- Stomach Issues: Stress can cause nausea,

stomachaches, or digestive problems.

- Sleep Problems: Trouble falling asleep, staying asleep, or waking up too early can be signs that stress is interfering with your rest.

- Changes in Appetite: Stress can cause you to eat more than usual (comfort eating) or lose your appetite altogether.
- Procrastination: If you find yourself putting off tasks because they seem too overwhelming, stress could be the culprit.
- withdrawal from Friends and Activities: When stress becomes too much, you might start to pull away from social activities or friends that you usually enjoy.

Recognizing these signs is crucial. Once you're aware of how stress is affecting you, it becomes easier to take steps to manage it.

TECHNIQUES FOR STRESS MANAGEMENT

Managing stress effectively is all about finding the right strategies that work for you. There's no one-size-fits-all solution, but there are several techniques that can help you take control of your stress and improve your overall well-being. One of the most effective ways to manage stress is through mindfulness and relaxation activities. Mindfulness is the practice of being fully present in the moment, without judgment. It's about paying attention to what's happening right now, rather than worrying about the past or the future. This can be as simple as focusing on your breath, noticing the sensations in your body, or paying attention to your surroundings. By practicing mindfulness regularly, you can train your mind to stay calm and focused, even in stressful situations. Meditation is another powerful tool for managing stress. It involves sitting quietly and focusing your mind on a single point of reference, such as your breath, a word, or a sound. Meditation helps to calm your mind, reduce anxiety, and improve your ability to handle stress. Even just a few minutes of meditation each day can make a big difference in how you feel.

Progressive muscle relaxation is a technique that involves tensing and then slowly releasing each muscle group in your body, starting from your toes and working your way up to your head. This practice helps to release physical tension and can be particularly helpful if stress is causing you to feel tight or sore. Guided imagery and visualization are also effective relaxation techniques. This involves imagining yourself in a peaceful place, like a beach or a forest, and using all your senses to make the scene as vivid as possible. This mental escape can help reduce stress and promote relaxation, even if you're in the middle of a hectic day. Another important aspect of stress management is the power of organization and time management. When you're organized, you can reduce the chaos in your life and feel more in control. Start by creating a daily schedule that includes everything you need to do, from homework to chores to social activities. Prioritize your tasks and break them down into manageable steps. This can help you stay on top of your responsibilities without feeling overwhelmed.

Using a planner or digital tools to keep track of your tasks and deadlines can also help you stay organized. Set reminders for important dates and check your planner regularly to make sure you're staying on track. By staying organized, you can reduce the stress that comes from feeling like you're always playing catch-up. Breaking tasks into smaller steps is another effective time management strategy. Large tasks can feel overwhelming, but by breaking them down into smaller, more manageable steps, you can make them less daunting. Focus on completing one step at a time, and before you know it, you'll have made significant progress. Prioritizing your to-do list is also key. Not everything on your list is equally important, so take the time to figure out which tasks need to be done first and which can wait. By focusing on the most important tasks first, you can reduce the stress of feeling like you have too much to do.As we've identified the sources and signs of stress, let's dive into some techniques to help you manage it. Remember, stress is a normal part of life, but it doesn't have to control your life. with the right tools, you can keep it in check and even turn it into a positive force that drives you to succeed.

MINDFULNESS AND RELAXATION AC-TIVITIES

Mindfulness is all about being present in the moment. It's a powerful way to reduce stress because it helps you to focus on the here and now, rather than worrying about the past or future. Here are some mindfulness techniques you can try:

- Deep Breathing: Take slow, deep breaths, focusing on the sensation of your breath as it enters and leaves your body. This simple act can calm your mind and reduce stress almost instantly.
- Meditation: Find a quiet place to sit, close your eyes, and focus on your breathing or a specific word or phrase. Meditation helps to clear your mind and can reduce feelings of stress.
- Progressive Muscle Relaxation: Starting from your toes and working up to your head, tense each muscle group for a few seconds and then relax. This technique helps release physical tension and promotes relaxation.
- Guided Imagery: Imagine yourself in a peaceful, calming place, like a beach or a forest. Close your eyes and use your senses to make the scene as vivid as possible. This can help distract you from stress and create a sense of calm.

THE POWER OF ORGANIZATION AND TIME MANAGEMENT

One of the best ways to reduce stress is by getting organized and managing your time effectively. When you're organized, you can stay on top of your tasks, avoid last-minute cramming, and feel more in control of your life.

- Create a Schedule: Write down all your tasks, assignments, and activities in a planner or on a calendar. Break down big tasks into smaller, more manageable ones, and set deadlines for each.
- Prioritize Your Tasks: Focus on the most important or time-sensitive tasks first. Use a system like the Eisenhower Matrix to decide what needs to be done immediately, what can wait, what can be delegated, and what can be eliminated.
- Avoid Procrastination: Start tasks as soon as possible, even if you only work on them for a short time. This will reduce the stress of trying to finish everything at the last minute.
- Keep Your Space Organized: A cluttered space can lead to a cluttered mind. Keep your room, backpack, and study area tidy to create a more peaceful environment.

Seeking Support and Assistance

It's important to recognize when you need support and to feel comfortable asking for it. Talking to someone you trust, like a friend, family member, or mentor, can be incredibly helpful. Sometimes, just sharing what you're going through can lighten the load. The person you talk to might offer advice, but often, the simple act of listening is enough to make you feel better. They can provide a fresh perspective, remind you that you're not alone, and offer the emotional support you need. If you're struggling with stress that seems unmanageable, it might be helpful to talk to a counselor or therapist. These professionals are trained to help you understand and manage your stress in healthy ways. They can offer strategies and tools tailored to your specific situation and help you work through any underlying issues that might be contributing to your stress. Seeking professional help is a proactive step toward taking control of your mental health and well-being.

Support groups can also be a valuable resource. These are groups of people who are going through similar experiences and come together to share their stories, offer support, and learn from each other. Being part of a support group can help you feel less isolated and provide you with practical advice and encouragement. School counselors can be another source of support. They understand the pressures that students face and can offer guidance on managing stress related to academics, social issues, and future planning. Don't hesitate to reach out to your school counselor if you're feeling overwhelmed—they're there to help you. Building a strong support network is also important. Surround yourself with people who care about you and are there to support you, whether it's friends, family, teachers, or mentors.

Having a network of supportive people can make a big difference in how you cope with stress. They can offer advice, provide a listening ear, or simply be there to comfort you during tough times. It's also important to remember that it's okay to ask for help with practical matters. If you're feeling overwhelmed with schoolwork or other responsibilities, don't hesitate to ask for help. Whether it's getting extra help from a teacher, asking a friend to study with you, or delegating tasks to others, reaching out for assistance can alleviate some of the pressure you're feeling.

KNOWING WHEN TO REACH OUT FOR SUPPORT

You don't have to go through stressful times alone. Knowing when and how to seek support is a sign of strength, not weakness. Whether it's talking to a friend, reaching out to a family member, or seeking professional help, there are many ways to get the support you need. No one should have to face stress alone, and sometimes the best way to manage it is by seeking support from others. Knowing when to reach out for help is a sign of strength, not weakness. There are times when stress becomes too much to handle on your own, and that's okay. It's okay to ask for help when you're feeling overwhelmed. Here are some signs that it might be time to reach out:

- Your stress is affecting your daily life: If stress is making it hard for you to function, whether it's at school, home, or with friends, it's time to get some help.
- You feel like you can't cope: If you're struggling to manage your stress despite trying different techniques, talking to someone can provide relief and new strategies.
- You're feeling isolated: If stress is causing you to withdraw from others, reaching out can help you reconnect and feel less alone.

BUILDING A STRONG SUPPORT SYSTEM

Creating a personalized stress management plan can be incredibly beneficial in helping you navigate the ups and downs of life. This plan is all about identifying what works best for you and having a set of strategies in place to use whenever you start to feel overwhelmed. Start by identifying your main sources of stress. Write them down and be specific. For example, instead of just writing "school," think about what aspects of school are causing you stress. Is it a particular subject, a looming deadline, or pressure to get good grades? Once you have a clear understanding of your stressors, you can start to think about how to address them. Next, list the stress management techniques that you find most helpful. Maybe it's deep breathing, going for a walk, or listening to music. Include a variety of strategies so you have different options depending on the situation. It's also helpful to think about which techniques work best in which scenarios. For example, deep breathing might be great when you're feeling anxious during a test, while taking a break to go for a walk might be more helpful when you're feeling overwhelmed by a big project. It's also important to include strategies for maintaining your overall well-being. This might include regular exercise, healthy eating, getting enough sleep, and making time for activities that you enjoy.

Taking care of your physical health is closely linked to managing stress, so don't overlook these important aspects of your plan. Having a plan for when stress becomes too much to handle on your own is also key. Identify who you can reach out to for support, whether it's a friend, family member, or counselor. Knowing that you have people to turn to can provide comfort and reassurance, even when you're not actively seeking help. Finally, make a commitment to yourself to use your stress management plan regularly. It's easy to let these strategies fall by the wayside when life gets busy, but by making stress management a priority, you're taking an important step toward maintaining your mental health and well-being. Having a strong support system is crucial for managing stress. Here are some ways to build and maintain one:

- Talk to Friends and Family: Share your feelings with people you trust. They might be able to offer advice, help you see things from a different perspective, or simply provide a listening ear.
- Join a Club or Group: Connecting with others who share your interests can provide a sense of community and belonging. Whether it's a sports team, a book club, or a volunteer group, being part of something can help reduce stress.
- Seek Professional Help: If stress becomes unmanageable, consider talking to a counselor or therapist. They can help you explore your feelings, develop coping strategies, and provide support in a safe, non-judgmental environment.

CONCLUSION: EMBRACING CALM IN A BUSY WORLD

Managing stress is an ongoing process, but it's one that you can master with practice. By understanding your stressors, recognizing the signs of being overwhelmed, and using techniques like mindfulness, organization, and seeking support, you can embrace calm even in a busy world. Remember, it's okay to take a step back, breathe, and take care of yourself. You deserve peace, and with the right tools, you can create it in your life.

Chapter 7

Creating and Maintaining Healthy Boundaries

As you reach the final chapter of this guide, it's essential to take a moment to reflect on how far you've come. The journey of self-discovery, overcoming challenges, and embracing self-love is not a straight path but a winding road filled with highs and lows. Yet, each step, no matter how small, has contributed to the person you are today. Reflecting on your growth isn't just about recognizing the changes you've made but also about understanding the depth of your experiences. Think about the moments when you doubted yourself but chose to move forward anyway. Consider the times when you confronted your fears, stood up for yourself, or simply decided to be kinder to yourself. These moments are milestones in your journey. Reflection allows you to see the patterns in your life, the lessons learned, and the strengths you've developed. It helps you connect the dots between your past and present, offering insight into your personal growth. For instance, you might realize that an experience you once viewed as a failure was actually a turning point that led to newfound resilience or wisdom. As you reflect, it's important to acknowledge that growth is not always linear. There may have been times when you felt like you were taking steps backward, but even these moments are part of the journey. They teach you about patience, perseverance, and the importance of self-compassion.

Remember, growth is about progress, not perfection. To fully appreciate your journey, you might consider journaling about your experiences. Write down the challenges you've faced, the victories you've celebrated, and the lessons you've learned along the way. This practice not only solidifies your understanding of your growth but also serves as a powerful reminder of your strength and resilience. Another meaningful way to reflect on your journey is to engage in a creative activity that allows you to express your emotions and insights. This could be through art, music, poetry, or any other medium that resonates with you. Creative expression can be a cathartic and healing process, helping you process your experiences and celebrate your growth in a deeply personal way. As you look back on your journey, don't forget to give yourself credit for the hard work you've done. It's easy to downplay your achievements, but every step you've taken toward self-love and self-acceptance is worth celebrating. You've shown courage, strength, and determination, and that deserves recognition. Reflecting on your growth also involves recognizing the support you've received along the way. Whether it's from friends, family, mentors, or even the inspiration you've drawn from books, podcasts, or other resources, acknowledging these sources of support is important. They have played a role in your journey, and expressing gratitude for them can deepen your sense of connection and fulfillment. As the poet Rainer Maria Rilke once said, "The only journey is the one within." This quote encapsulates the essence of your self-love journey. It's a journey of inner exploration, growth, and transformation. By taking the time to reflect on your growth, you honor the path you've walked and prepare yourself for the road ahead.

The Importance of Setting Boundaries

Boundaries are like the invisible fences we put around ourselves to protect our emotional, physical, and mental well-being. Think of them as the rules we set in our personal lives to ensure that we feel safe, respected, and understood. Just as we wouldn't let someone walk into our room without knocking, we shouldn't allow others to cross into our personal space—whether it's our emotions, our time, or our body—without our permission. Setting boundaries is essential because it helps us define who we are, what we value, and what we need from others. It's about telling the world, "This is where I end, and you begin." without boundaries, we might find ourselves feeling overwhelmed, disrespected, or even resentful because others are taking more from us than we are comfortable giving. Boundaries are not about building walls to shut people out; instead, they are about creating guidelines to let people in, but only to the extent that we feel comfortable and safe.

UNDERSTANDING WHY BOUNDARIES ARE ESSENTIAL

The world around us is filled with expectations, from schoolwork to friendships, family obligations, and social media. It can sometimes feel like everyone wants a piece of us, and without boundaries, we can quickly become stretched too thin. Boundaries are essential because they allow us to manage our time, energy, and emotions in a way that is healthy and sustainable. They help us avoid burnout and ensure that we are giving to others from a place of fullness, rather than depletion. When we understand the importance of boundaries, we start to see them as acts of self-respect. They are a way of saying, "I matter, my needs matter, and I deserve to be treated with respect." Boundaries also teach others how to treat us; they set the standard for what is acceptable behavior in our relationships. without them, people might inadvertently or intentionally take advantage of us, not because they are bad people, but because we haven't communicated what we need.

RECOGNIZING PERSONAL LIMITS

Recognizing our personal limits is the first step in setting boundaries. Everyone has different thresholds for what they can handle, and these limits can vary depending on the situation. For example, you might have a high tolerance for stress when it comes to schoolwork but a low tolerance for drama in friendships. Understanding where your limits lie helps you identify when a boundary needs to be set. Personal limits are often discovered through experience. You might not realize that a particular situation makes you uncomfortable until you're in the middle of it. It's important to listen to your feelings and pay attention to any discomfort or unease. These emotions are your mind's way of telling you that something isn't right, and that a boundary may need to be established. Recognizing personal limits also means acknowledging that it's okay to say "no." Many of us struggle with saying no because we don't want to disappoint others or seem selfish. However, saying no is a powerful way to honor your boundaries and protect your well-being. It's a reminder that you have the right to prioritize yourself and that doing so is not only okay but necessary.

HOW BOUNDARIES SAFEGUARD YOUR WELLBEING

Boundaries are essential for safeguarding your well-being. They protect you from overcommitting, from being emotionally drained, and from being taken advantage of. When you set boundaries, you are taking control of your life and ensuring that you are in charge of your own happiness. For example, let's say you have a friend who constantly asks for favors but never reciprocates. This friend might not even realize that their behavior is causing you stress because you've never set a boundary. By gently letting them know that you're not always available to help, you protect your time and energy, allowing yourself the space to recharge. Boundaries also safeguard your mental health. In relationships, whether with friends, family, or romantic partners, clear boundaries prevent misunderstandings and reduce the likelihood of conflict. They help ensure that you feel respected and valued, which in turn boosts your self-esteem. When you know that your boundaries are being honored, you can relax and enjoy your relationships without the fear of being hurt or taken for granted.

Communicating Your Boundaries with Kindness

Communicating boundaries can feel challenging, especially if you're not used to asserting yourself. However, it's important to remember that setting boundaries is not about being harsh or unfriendly; it's about being clear and honest with others about what you need. When communicating your boundaries, it's helpful to use "I" statements, which focus on your feelings and needs rather than blaming the other person. For example, instead of saying, "You always interrupt me," you could say, "I feel unheard when I'm interrupted, and I would appreciate it if I could finish speaking before you respond." This approach is less likely to make the other person feel defensive and more likely to lead to a positive outcome. It's also important to be consistent with your boundaries. Once you've communicated them, stick to them. This might mean reminding others of your boundaries from time to time, especially if they're not used to you asserting yourself. It's okay to reinforce your boundaries and to expect that others will respect them.

TECHNIQUES FOR ASSERTIVE AND RESPECTFUL COMMUNICATION

Assertive communication is key to setting and maintaining boundaries. Being assertive means expressing your thoughts, feelings, and needs in a way that is clear, direct, and respectful. It's about standing up for yourself without being aggressive or passive. One technique for assertive communication is the "broken record" technique. This involves calmly and consistently repeating your boundary until the other person understands and respects it. For example, if someone keeps pressuring you to do something you're not comfortable with, you can keep repeating, "I've decided not to, but thank you for understanding," until they stop pushing. Another technique is to practice saying no in a firm but polite way. This might feel uncomfortable at first, especially if you're used to saying yes to avoid conflict. However, with practice, it will become easier. Remember, you don't need to provide a lengthy explanation for your boundaries. A simple, "No, I'm not available," or "No, I don't feel comfortable doing that," is sufficient. Finally, it's important to listen actively to the other person's response. Setting boundaries is not just about stating your needs; it's also about being open to dialogue and finding a solution that works for both parties. Active listening shows that you respect the other person's perspective, even if you don't agree with it.

OVERCOMING OBSTACLES AND MAINTAIN- ING LIMITS

Setting boundaries is one thing, but maintaining them is another challenge altogether. People might test your boundaries, either intentionally or unintentionally, and it's up to you to stand firm. This can be difficult, especially if you're dealing with someone who is used to you not having boundaries or who reacts negatively to your new boundaries. One of the biggest obstacles to maintaining boundaries is guilt. You might feel guilty for saying no, for prioritizing yourself, or for potentially disappointing others. It's important to remember that setting boundaries is not selfish; it's an act of self-care. You have a right to protect your well-being, and those who truly care about you will respect that. Another obstacle is fear of conflict. It's natural to want to avoid conflict, but avoiding it by not setting boundaries can lead to resentment and frustration. It's better to address issues head-on, even if it leads to a temporary disagreement, than to allow them to fester and damage your relationships in the long run. To maintain your boundaries, it's helpful to remind yourself why you set them in the first place. Keep in mind the positive impact that boundaries have on your life and well-being. If someone challenges your boundaries, respond calmly but firmly, and don't be afraid to walk away from a situation if your boundaries are not being respected.

Boundaries in Different Relationships

Boundaries look different depending on the type of relationship. In friendships, boundaries might involve how much time you spend together, what topics you're comfortable discussing, and how you handle conflicts. For example, you might set a boundary around not gossiping or not tolerating disrespectful behavior.

RELATIONSHIPS WITH FRIENDS, FAMILY, AND LOVE

In family relationships, boundaries can be more complex, especially if you're dealing with parents or siblings who are used to a certain dynamic. It might involve setting limits on how much you share about your personal life, how you handle family obligations, or how you communicate your needs. In romantic relationships, boundaries are crucial for maintaining a healthy balance between intimacy and independence. This might involve setting boundaries around physical affection, communication, and how you spend your time together and apart. It's important to discuss these boundaries openly with your partner to ensure that both of you feel comfortable and respected.

FINDING A BALANCE BETWEEN AUTONOMY AND CONNECTION

Setting boundaries doesn't mean cutting yourself off from others; it's about finding a balance between your needs for autonomy and connection. Autonomy is your ability to make your own choices and live your life according to your values and desires. Connection, on the other hand, is your need for closeness, support, and relationships with others. The key is to find a balance where you feel free to be yourself and pursue your goals, while also maintaining meaningful connections with the people who matter to you. This balance might look different for everyone, and it can change over time as your needs and circumstances evolve. For example, you might need more autonomy when you're focused on a big project or going through a challenging time. During these periods, it's okay to set stronger boundaries around your time and energy. On the other hand, you might crave more connection during times of celebration or when you're feeling lonely. Being flexible with your boundaries allows you to adjust to your current needs while still honoring your core values.

CONCLUSION: HONORING YOUR NEEDS AND VALUES

Setting and maintaining healthy boundaries is one of the most empowering things you can do for yourself. It's a way of honoring your needs, your values, and your well-being. Boundaries allow you to live authentically, to give from a place of abundance rather than depletion, and to build relationships that are based on mutual respect and understanding. As you navigate your teenage years and beyond, remember that boundaries are not a one-time thing; they are an ongoing practice. It's okay to adjust your boundaries as you grow and as your needs change. The important thing is to stay true to yourself and to remember that you deserve to be treated with

kindness, respect, and care. Setting boundaries is not always easy, but it is always worth it. It might take time, practice, and courage, but with each boundary you set, you are taking a step towards a life that is more balanced, fulfilling, and true to who you are.

Conclusion To This Book

Recap of Your Empowering Journey

As you reflect on your journey through this book, take a moment to celebrate the path you've walked. From the first page, you embarked on a quest of self-discovery, embracing the ups and downs, the challenges, and the victories that come with growing into your authentic self. You've learned to look within, to understand your emotions, to honor your needs, and to embrace your unique beauty. This journey wasn't just about reading words on a page; it was about transformation—building a relationship with yourself that is rooted in kindness, respect, and love. Through the chapters, you've explored the concept of self-love in its many forms. You've discovered that self-love isn't just about pampering yourself with bubble baths or treating yourself to something special, although those things are wonderful.

True self-love is about nurturing your inner world—accepting yourself fully, forgiving yourself when you falter, and cheering yourself on through life's challenges. It's about recognizing your worth and knowing that you deserve to be treated with the same kindness and respect that you extend to others. Each exercise, reflection, and story you engaged with was a step toward a deeper understanding of yourself. You've faced your fears, questioned limiting beliefs, and opened your heart to new ways of thinking. These are the seeds of growth that will continue to flourish as you move forward. Your journey of self-love is ongoing, and with each passing day, you are becoming more aligned with the person you are meant to be.

CELEBRATING YOUR GROWTH AND ACHIEVEMENTS

Take a moment to reflect on all that you've achieved. The progress you've made may not always be visible, but it is real and significant. Perhaps you've noticed a shift in how you speak to yourself—less criticism and more compassion. Maybe you've started setting healthier boundaries, or you've become more comfortable expressing your needs. These are all signs of growth, and they deserve to be celebrated. Your achievements are not just in the big moments, but also in the small, everyday choices you make. Choosing to show up for yourself, even when it's difficult, is an achievement. Deciding to forgive yourself for past mistakes is an achievement. Every time you choose to believe in your worth, you are achieving something remarkable. Your growth is a testament to your strength, resilience, and commitment to yourself. As you celebrate your progress, remember that growth is not linear. There will be days when you feel on top of the world, and days when self-doubt creeps in. Both are part of the journey.

What matters is that you continue to move forward, even if it's just one small step at a time. You are on a path of continuous growth, and every experience you encounter is an opportunity to learn and evolve.

EMBRACING THE JOURNEY OF SELF-LOVE

Self-love is not a destination; it's a lifelong journey. There will always be more to learn about yourself, more ways to grow, and more opportunities to practice self-compassion. Embrace this journey with an open heart and a willingness to explore. Understand that there will be challenges along the way, but also know that you have the tools and inner strength to navigate them. Embracing self-love means accepting yourself exactly as you are in this moment, while also recognizing that you have the power to change and grow. It's about being gentle with yourself when you stumble, and celebrating yourself when you succeed. It's about learning to trust yourself, to listen to your intuition, and to honor your feelings. As you continue on this journey, remember that self-love is not about perfection. It's about being authentically you—flaws, quirks, and all. It's about showing up for yourself, even when it's hard. and it's about knowing that you are worthy of love, simply because you exist.

ENCOURAGEMENT TO KEEP GROWING AND LEARNING

Your journey doesn't end here; in fact, it's just beginning. The insights and skills you've gained are the foundation for a lifetime of growth and learning. Keep seeking out new knowledge, whether it's through books, conversations, experiences, or introspection. Every day is an opportunity to learn something new about yourself and the world around you. Remember that growth is not about reaching a final goal, but about continually evolving. Be curious about your thoughts and feelings, and be open to new perspectives. Surround yourself with people who uplift and inspire you, and who encourage you to keep growing. Seek out experiences that challenge you and help you expand your horizons. As you continue to grow, be patient with yourself. Change takes time, and it's okay if progress feels slow at times. What matters is that you keep moving forward, no matter how small the steps may seem. Trust that every step you take is bringing you closer to a deeper understanding of yourself and a more fulfilling life.

FINAL WORDS OF ENCOURAGEMENT

You are on a beautiful journey, and there is so much ahead for you to explore and discover. As you continue on this path, remember to be kind to yourself. Treat yourself with the same love and compassion that you would offer to a dear friend. Celebrate your successes, learn from your challenges, and always believe in your worth. You have the power to create a life that is full of love, joy, and fulfillment. It all starts with how you treat yourself. Continue to prioritize your well-being, nurture your dreams, and honor your unique path. Know that you are enough, just as you are, and that you have everything you need within you to live a life of love and purpose. Embrace every step of your journey with love and compassion. The road ahead may not always be easy, but it is yours to walk, and it is filled with endless possibilities. You are capable, you are deserving, and you are loved. Keep shining your light, and remember that the most important relationship you will ever have is the one you have with yourself.

Appendices

WORKSHEETS AND EXERCISES

Self-Reflection Prompts

- What are three things I love about myself?
- When was the last time I felt truly proud of myself, and why?
- What are some limiting beliefs I hold, and how can I challenge them?
- How do I typically speak to myself, and how can I be more compassionate in my self-talk?
- What does self-love mean to me, and how can I practice it daily?

Goal-Setting and Planning Sheets

- Vision Board Worksheet – Create a visual representation of your goals and dreams. Cut out images and words that resonate with your vision and glue them onto a board. Place your vision board somewhere you'll see it daily as a reminder of where you're headed.
- SMART Goals Worksheet – Use this sheet to set Specific, Measurable, Achievable, Relevant, and Time-bound goals. Write down your goals and break them down into actionable steps.
- Daily Gratitude Journal – Start each day by writing down three things you're grateful for. This practice can help shift your focus to the positive and cultivate a mindset of abundance.

GLOSSARY OF TERMS

- Self-Compassion – Treating yourself with the same kindness, care, and understanding that you would offer to a friend in times of difficulty.

- Mindfulness - The practice of being fully present in the moment, without judgment, and with a sense of curiosity and openness.
- Limiting Beliefs - Negative thoughts or beliefs that constrain your potential and hinder your ability to achieve your goals.
- Emotional Intelligence - The ability to recognize, understand, manage, and reason with emotions in oneself and others.
- Boundaries - Personal limits you set in relationships to protect your well-being and ensure your needs are respected.
- Resilience - The capacity to recover quickly from difficulties and adapt to challenging situations.
- Self-Awareness - The conscious knowledge of your own character, feelings, motives, and desires.

As you reach the end of this book, take a moment to reflect on the incredible journey you've undertaken. Each page, each exercise, and each reflection has been a step toward discovering the depths of your own heart. You've begun to understand that self-love is not just a concept, but a way of living—a commitment to treating yourself with the same kindness, compassion, and respect that you so freely offer to others. In a world that often tells us we are not enough, you've chosen to believe in your own worth. This is no small feat; it's an act of courage, a declaration that you are deserving of love, happiness, and peace. There will be days when the world feels heavy, when self-doubt creeps in, and the path ahead seems unclear. On those days, I hope you remember the strength that lies within you. The strength to rise, to keep moving forward, and to hold yourself with the gentle compassion that you would offer to a dear friend. Self-love is not a destination, but a lifelong journey. It is a relationship that evolves, deepens, and grows with time. There will be moments of triumph, where you feel fully aligned with your true self, and moments of challenge, where old fears and doubts may resurface. But in every moment, you have the power to choose love—love for yourself, love for your journey, and love for the person you are becoming. This book was just the beginning.

As you continue to grow and evolve, remember that self-love is about embracing all parts of yourself—the light and the dark, the strengths and the imperfections. It's about being patient with yourself as you learn and grow, forgiving yourself when you stumble, and celebrating yourself when you succeed. It's about acknowledging that you are a work in progress, and that is something to be proud of. Take with you the lessons you've learned, and let them guide you in the days and years to come. Continue to explore what self-love means to you, and let it be the foundation upon which you build your life. Surround yourself with people who uplift you, pursue the things that bring you joy, and never stop striving to be the best version of yourself. But also, remember to rest, to take time to nurture your soul, and to be gentle with yourself along the way. You are a unique and beautiful soul, deserving of all the love and happiness the world has to offer. As you move forward, hold onto the belief that you are enough, just as you are. Trust in your journey, and know that you are exactly where you need to be. You have the strength, wisdom, and courage to create a life that is rich with meaning, purpose, and joy.

In the words of Buddha, "You yourself, as much as anybody in the entire universe, deserve your love and affection."

Let these words be a reminder to you, a guiding light on days when the path seems unclear. You are worthy of love—not because of what you do, but because of who you are. Embrace every step of your journey with love, compassion, and an open heart. The world is a better place because you are in it, and you are deserving of all the beauty and joy it has to offer. Keep shining your light, keep believing in yourself, and keep loving yourself fiercely and unconditionally. The best is yet to come.

Jacqueline D. Austin